IS

A PERSONAL HISTORY

RAMABHADRAN ARAVAMUDAN is an award-winning senior scientist who has been associated with the Indian space programme from its very inception. He has served as the director of the Satish Dhawan Space Centre at Sriharikota and of the ISRO Satellite Centre, Bengaluru.

GITA ARAVAMUDAN is a veteran journalist and author with several books and hundreds of articles to her credit.

ISRO
A PERSONAL HISTORY

R. ARAVAMUDAN
WITH
GITA ARAVAMUDAN

HarperCollins *Publishers* India

First published in India by
HarperCollins *Publishers* in 2017
A-75, Sector 57, Noida, Uttar Pradesh 201301, India
www.harpercollins.co.in

2 4 6 8 10 9 7 5 3

Copyright © R. Aravamudan and Gita Aravamudan 2017

P-ISBN: 978-93-5264-363-9
E-ISBN: 978-93-5264-364-6

Typeset in 11.5/15.1 Adobe Garamond at
Manipal Digital Systems, Manipal

Printed and bound at
Saurabh Printers Pvt.Ltd.

To all my colleagues at ISRO, present, past and future, my co-travellers on India's incredible journey into space

Contents

Prologue

28 September 2014

My laptop screen glowed with the colours of Mars. I could hardly believe it. We had done it! Mangalyan, India's first home-grown mission to Mars, was a spectacular success. I was actually looking at an image captured by the Mars Colour Camera (MCC) we had built and mounted on our own Mars Orbiter Mission (MOM).

MOM had been launched from Sriharikota ten months ago, on 5 November 2013. My wife Gita and I watched the spectacular take-off from the new state-of-the-art control centre. As ISRO's workhorse PSLV-C25 soared faultlessly into space, we anxiously watched the flight path on the monitor screen. But the men and women sitting at the consoles were cool and confident – the PSLV had proved itself over and over, and this generation had learnt to take it for granted. In any case, the launch was the least of their worries. They knew that over the next ten months they had the much more complicated task of guiding and safeguarding the 500 kg Mars Orbiter as it flew for almost a year through space.

And then they had to slide it into a precise orbit around a faraway planet. Almost all the ISRO centres were involved in this complex mission. Ground stations across the world were tracking it – finally, the eyes of the world were on us.

I was now witnessing the final spectacular success of that Mission. No other Mars Mission had succeeded in its very first attempt. ISRO had developed all the technology from scratch. And we had used so many innovative ideas for cost cutting and fuel saving. Now our success was splashed across space.

Thirty-five years ago when we anxiously watched the take-off of our first SLV, we could never even have imagined a mission of this scale.

10 August 1979

By the second half of the 1970s, we were on a high – we were getting ready to launch SLV-3, our first homegrown launch vehicle.

We were not a battle-hardened team of professionals with scores of successful rocket and satellite missions behind us. But we were young, highly motivated and hardworking. None of us had been part of an actual satellite launch, and now we were thirsting to realize our pre-flight dreams.

There were quite a few sceptics, in our midst and around us. Indians had never done such a thing on their own ever before, they said. What could a bunch of youngsters do? Besides, weren't we reinventing the wheel? But the organization and the government were solidly behind us, and supported our teams morally and materially.

Finally, a good five years after the date originally proposed by Dr Vikram Sarabhai, the SLV-3 was ready and assembled for flight on the pad at Sriharikota. Abdul Kalam, a close friend and colleague, was on tenterhooks. This was his first major project.

Whenever Kalam was asked to define the success criterion of the project, he would say that the very act of bringing the assembled vehicle on to the launch pad constituted 50 per cent success. He would go on to assign success percentages to various events, such as the take-off, first stage function, second stage function and so on until the actual injection into orbit of the satellite.

Would this, our first launch, score on all counts?

The launch was scheduled for the early morning and I was seated in the control room in front of a console, monitoring the status of the tracking systems the team had built from scratch and installed. Senior colleagues were anxiously watching the progress of the countdown from behind. Kalam was at the mission director's console, busily talking on the telephone to various subsystem specialists. The countdown clock was ticking and Kalam had given the mission director's clearance for the launch.

Things were moving smoothly. The umbilical cable was pulled out and the vehicle was on its own batteries. The countdown edged towards the dramatic last ten seconds. Right on the dot, at count zero, the first stage ignited and the vehicle majestically lifted off. Those of us involved with the launch were intent on our consoles and did not go out to see the take-off.

We heard the mighty roar of the vehicle a few seconds later as the sound took its time to reach us. The burning of the first stage seemed normal. I was watching Kalam for some sign. Had the rocket performed well? After some time, I saw a blank and fixed expression on his face, followed by disappointment. He turned around and made a thumbs-down gesture. Something had gone wrong.

The vehicle went out of control and splashed into the Bay of Bengal at a distance of 560 km from the coast, about five minutes after take-off. Our very first attempt to launch a satellite launch vehicle was a failure, although it was officially dubbed a 'partial success'.

1

The Beginning

I remember clearly the moment I decided I was going to be a rocket scientist.

The year was 1962. It was just another day at the reactor control division of the Department of Atomic Energy (DAE) in Trombay. The excitement of moving to Bombay from Madras and into a very sought-after job had worn off. After two years, my work at DAE had become routine and I was getting fed up of the crowds and the hustle and bustle. I was twenty-four. Restless. And wanting to move on.

I was chatting in the canteen with my friend, also a junior engineer like me. He told me he had heard that a scientist called Dr Vikram Sarabhai, founder of the Physical Research Laboratory (PRL) in Ahmedabad, was looking for volunteers to set up a rocket launch pad in south Kerala. He wanted to form a core group of young engineers who would be sent to the US to train at NASA before they were relocated to Kerala.

'Should we volunteer?' my friend asked pensively. 'It all sounds quite vague. But NASA sounds exciting.'

Even while he was wondering about it, I had made up my mind. This seemed like a heaven-sent opportunity. First NASA and then back home to south India. What more could I ask for? There was no question. I would try my luck – I was volunteering!

Thinking back now it seems almost dreamlike. No recruitment processes, no job interviews – nothing. The first recruits for India's space programme were all young volunteers like me from the premier scientific institutions of the day. And we all just heard about it by word of mouth.

After that everything happened in a rush. When they heard of my decision to volunteer, most of my colleagues thought I was mad. Why on earth would I want to sacrifice a career with steady growth prospects to chase a chimera? I had been directly recruited into DAE after graduating with a first rank from the Madras Institute of Technology, one of the country's most prestigious engineering colleges in those days. And now I wanted to throw it all away?

The only safety net I had was the fact that the programme was being backed by DAE, so I would continue to be on their payrolls. When I talked to my parents back home they were more concerned about my pay packet. Would I be able to sustain myself? We were a middle-class family and money did not exactly grow on trees. But when they realized how thrilled I was at the thought of going to NASA, they supported me. After all, what was the worst that could happen? I might not be chosen. And if the project failed, I could still go back to my old job as this would be a project done on deputation.

And so it was that I packed my small suitcase and took an overnight train to Ahmedabad to meet Sarabhai. With me was another young volunteer. We would both be interviewed by the man himself, and if we were chosen we would have to leave for the US within a month.

Within the intervening two weeks since I heard of this opportunity, I had found out all I could about Vikram Sarabhai. I knew he was in his forties and the son of the great textile industrialist Ambalal Sarabhai. Although he came from a very rich business family, he had decided to pursue a career in physics. He was a student of the legendary Sir C.V. Raman. After getting a degree from Cambridge he had set up PRL in Ahmedabad, already a hub of scientific research in India.

Vikram Sarabhai was now spearheading a project envisioned by a consortium of scientists from across the globe. They wanted to study the magnetic equator using small sounding rockets. The magnetic equator is, like its cousin the geographical equator, an imaginary line around the earth where its magnetic field becomes horizontal. It lies very close to the geographical equator. Scientists from all over the world wanted to launch rocket payloads from this region because they wished to study a rather unique phenomenon: a strong belt of charged particles called the 'electro jet' which run above the magnetic equator and have a great impact on worldwide radio communication. The study of this phenomenon could only be carried out from under the magnetic equator by launching instruments carried by sounding rockets.

Sites on the Kerala tip were found the best suited for locating such a rocket launching station. After inspecting several possible locations, Sarabhai and his advisors had zeroed in on Thumba, a small fishermen's beach close to Trivandrum, the capital of Kerala.

I did not know all these details, of course, when I set off for Ahmedabad. In fact, I just had a very hazy idea of rockets and rocket launches. But the prospect was exciting.

From the railway station my friend and I took a rickshaw to Navrangpura where PRL was situated. While we waited nervously at the reception a handsome young man came up and greeted us warmly. He introduced himself as E.V. Chitnis, a colleague of Dr Sarabhai's. Vikram was on his way, he said, and asked us to sit down and make ourselves comfortable.

About an hour later, we were still hanging around in the corridor, waiting, when a Standard Herald car with an open top stopped at the portico. A dashing man in his forties, dressed in white shorts and shirt, stepped out. It took us a couple of minutes to realize that this was the famous Dr Sarabhai himself! He was so informal. He greeted us with a cheery hello and bundled us into his car. We drove a short distance to a telemetry receiving trailer from NASA parked in the campus.

Sarabhai's charm was almost mesmeric. Within moments we were totally absorbed in his explanation of how this trailer received signals from satellites. He told us he was planning to do scientific experiments from Kerala, perhaps from near Trivandrum, using rockets carrying measuring instruments.

Telemetry and tracking would be very vital components of the rocket range, he said, and one of the chosen persons would be trained in this. He also described the launch pad, telemetry receiving station, radar and Doppler velocity and position system he hoped to install.

It all sounded like science fiction to me. By now I was bowled over by the charisma of Dr Sarabhai, the gleam in his eyes when he described his plans and his sincerity. I wanted very much to be one of the chosen few.

Back at work in Bombay, I was on tenterhooks for the next couple of days. Would I be chosen? I had no clue, nothing to go by, since there had been no formal interview, no written test. I was preparing myself for the worst. I would have to continue with my rather boring job with reactor control. My friends at South India Concerns, the lodge where I stayed, tried to console me. 'Better to have a steady job than chase some idealistic scientist's dream,' they said.

I had almost lost all hope when the news came. I had been selected! The other engineer who came with me had unfortunately not made it. I was excited but now my euphoria was tempered by my colleagues at DAE who kept cautioning me about giving up my comfortable job. This rocket programme was uncertain, they said, and could fold up anytime. I should wait for it to get properly established before I took the jump. But my mind was made up – I was going.

Before finally signing up, I had to submit a letter to my boss Dr A.S. Rao who was at the administrative office at the Old Yacht Club near India Gate. I still remember that rather unnerving meeting very well. I nervously entered the room where he was sitting with a couple of other senior scientists, including the legendary Dr Raja Ramanna who was still a fairly young man then. I gave him my letter.

'So you have decided to go!' he remarked.

'What do you think?' I asked, mustering up all my courage. 'Do you think this project will succeed?'

Raja Ramanna replied on his behalf.

'We are not astrologers!' he laughed. 'How can we predict what will happen?' He took my letter and read it. 'Well, you have to take a risk. All the best!' And he handed the letter back to my boss.

Since the facility at Thumba had not come up yet, all the arrangements for my US trip had to be done under the aegis of DAE, which proceeded with all governmental formalities for issuing the deputation order and other travel arrangements. The first batch of trainees was to leave for the US in December 1962. I was the only government employee. The other three people recruited at the same time were B. Ramakrishna Rao, P.P. Kale and A.S. Prakasa Rao. They were all employees of PRL, which at that time was a private organization.

I was to report at the sounding rocket branch of NASA's Goddard Space Flight Centre at Beltsville, Maryland, which was just a few kilometres from Washington, DC. December weather at Washington, DC, would be severe, I was warned, and told to be prepared with warm clothing. I had always lived in the warm climates of Madras or Bombay and I did not even know what real cold weather meant! And, here I was, about to land in DC in the peak of winter. Fortunately the government rules provided for some equipment allowance and I got myself two woollen suits made to order from one of the better-known tailors of Bombay. I also bought some woollen pullovers and woollen socks.

At that time no one from my immediate family had travelled abroad; for them I was a trailblazer. Since I did not have enough time to go down to Madras to say goodbye, my father decided he would come over to Bombay to see me off. I was sharing an apartment with a friend in Wadala and my father stayed with me. He joined a small group of friends and colleagues who formed the send-off party at the Santa Cruz airport. Those were the days when people could even walk across the tarmac to bid goodbye! But since this was an international flight I had to go through immigration and customs and pass through the departure lounge. I was feeling quite nervous. Although I had sent cables to the NASA authorities I was not sure what was in store. Apart from that first meeting with Sarabhai I had not met him again and all further instructions were through other persons.

Meanwhile, the other three people from PRL had already reached the US a few days ahead and had made contact with NASA. They had temporarily checked into a hotel pending permanent arrangements. Landing at DC after a long and arduous journey with virtually no sleep for almost thirty-six hours, I heaved a huge sigh of relief when I saw the chubby figure of B. Ramakrishna Rao waiting at the arrival lounge. I remembered having met him on my sole visit to PRL for the interview with Dr Sarabhai. At that time he had not yet joined the programme but had been very friendly and showed me around the campus.

Now I found Ramakrishna Rao had managed to commandeer a NASA limousine and we drove in style straight to the hotel where we were to stay. For the first time ever in my life I saw snow all over the roads and experienced the sudden drop in temperature from the 30°C of Bombay to the near zero degrees of Washington, DC. The limousine chauffeur was amused by my reaction. He asked me whether this was my first time in the US and commented on my good English!

Thirty-one-year-old Ramakrishna Rao, who had an ME in electronics, was the oldest amongst the four of us. He was already married and had a child. Prakash Rao and I were twenty-four and Kale, who was in his very early twenties, was still an MSc student. The three of us were single. Prakash Rao had finished his MSc and joined PRL as a research student and Kale, the son of a senior executive of Sarabhai's company, had a great aptitude for space research. Ramakrishna Rao, also from PRL was a last-minute addition to the team. Our project was to build a telemetry ground station mounted inside a trailer which, after testing and validation, would be shipped to Thumba for installation. This was to be on long-term loan to Thumba but would remain the property of NASA.

Our hotel was in the heart of Washington, DC, and on our first day at Beltsville, we were picked up by a NASA car and taken to the sounding rocket division which was actually located in the Maryland state, about 10 km from the city. We were received by Ed Bissell who was to be our training guide and were taken to our office room and introduced to the staff around.

Bissell had found us a two-bedroom apartment at a walking distance from our workplace at a very reasonable rent. He also got us a second-hand Chevrolet car for $50 that was perfectly roadworthy and even had a heater and radio! NASA gave us a daily allowance of $16 which was a princely sum even in 1963. We were actually able to save the bulk of it. We soon equipped the kitchen and began making our own meals. Two of us could drive and we used to drive around in the city and do our own shopping. Weekends were reserved for sightseeing and downtown visits.

Ed Bissell had rechristened all of us. On our first meeting he tried very hard but couldn't get our names right. Kale became Kale as in 'gale'. He gave up on me and just picked up the last three letters of my name. So I became Dan. And the other two were Senior and Junior, as in Rao senior and Rao junior.

In all the excitement of arriving, I had forgotten to inform my parents about my safe journey. A week or two after I settled down I posted a long letter to my father describing my new life. That letter took its own time to reach. Meanwhile, my father became panicky and sent an urgent cable to NASA asking about me. The NASA officials in turn got worried and so one day I was summoned urgently to Bissell's office where I found some people from the headquarters waiting for me. I got a scare. But they were actually very kind and concerned.

'Send a cable to your father immediately, young man,' one of them said. 'Your old man is really worried.'

One day when the rest of us were a little late turning up for work, one of the guys at NASA asked Ramakrishna Rao, 'Where are your buddies?' The term was new to us and so we started jocularly calling each other 'Buddy'. But finally the name Buddy stuck to Ramakrishna Rao, and just as I came to be known as 'Dan' throughout the Indian Space Research Organisation (ISRO), he became universally known as 'Buddy'.

Buddy and I had the longest stint in the US. We reached on a cold December day in 1962 and left on an equally freezing morning in December 1963. But that one year was a packed and eventful one. All the others in our group had left by then. Our stay was extended because Sarabhai wanted us to be trained in radar and telemetry tracking.

To start with, the four of us were assigned to work at Beltsville in Washington, DC. We were very close to the University of Maryland. The Goddard Space Centre to which this unit was attached focused on launching and tracking sounding rockets. Beltsville was a fairly small unit with less than a hundred people working on the assembly of payloads and data analysis. We would sometimes go over to the main Goddard Centre to collect parts or to observe some assemblies. Our NASA office had no cafeteria but had facilities for making coffee. At lunchtime there would be a siren; a chuck wagon carrying food would arrive and all of us would troop out to buy sandwiches.

Unlike ISRO, NASA has traditionally involved the private sector in all its programmes. Consequently, all the major rockets and satellites were designed and built in the laboratories of the huge multinational conglomerates who partnered with this premier space agency. This also meant that we were not exposed to the technology that went into building the big rockets and satellites. No technology was transferred or acquired during this phase. In fact, the entire training offered to us by NASA was what was normally given to an operator or technician. We learned nothing related to design or engineering. No theory was taught, there was very little instruction, and we were mostly left to handle the equipment on our own. In retrospect I realize all our learning was done on our own after we returned!

Around March 1963 H.G.S. Murthy, D. Easwaradas and A.P.J. Abdul Kalam also arrived in the US. Murthy was in his mid-forties, was much older than us, married and with children. He had more than twenty years of work experience, although obviously not in this field. He had worked in Hindustan Aeronautics Limited (HAL) as an engineer for a number of years before joining a defence weapons testing range. Sarabhai picked him up because he had experience in the testing of carbines and other explosives. He was to take over as a test director for the sounding rocket launches.

Easwaradas, in his late twenties, was recently married. He was a product of the first batch of the Atomic Energy Training School and had worked in the reactor engineering division of DAE for about three or four years before he opted for this new programme. Kalam who was in his early thirties was a bachelor. After passing out of the Madras Institute of Technology, he had worked at the Aeronautical Development Establishment (ADE) in Bangalore for about four years – he had even built a trial hovercraft in which he gave some VIPs a ride!

They spent a couple of days with us but were then sent off to NASA's sounding rocket launch station on Wallops Island in Virginia. They were to be trained in rocket assembly, launching and explosive safety. Murthy had some exposure to the overall planning of launches and the management of a rocket station. He was the first to leave. After about two months at Wallops Island, he had to return to Trivandrum to commence work on the construction of the Thumba Equatorial Rocket Launching Station (TERLS) along with ISRO's first civil engineer R.D. John.

Easwaradas, known as Das, and Kalam left for India after another month. The other four of us continued to work at Beltsville, but would visit Wallops to watch some typical launches. Kale and Prakasa Rao were trained in Doppler tracking and went back to India by about June–July 1963. Buddy and I stayed on and were moved to Wallops in mid-1963 along with our telemetry trailer. The idea was to try it out before it was shifted to Thumba. Once we moved to Wallops, Sarabhai decided we should get trained in radar tracking and a few other aspects of launching and so our stay got extended. So, all six of us were together at Wallops Island for just a couple of months.

Wallops Island was originally part of a military training centre and had its own hostel called the Bachelor Officers Quarters or BOQ. Our hostel had an attached cafeteria which served the entire range staff. We had all our meals there. The food was highly subsidized and we could pick up enough vegetarian stuff to keep us going. We lived mainly on mashed potatoes, boiled beans or peas, bread and lots of milk. Like the Americans we had dinner by about 5.30 pm. There was also a bar functioning in the evenings. But, although almost all of us were in our twenties, we never thought of going there. We all came from highly conservative backgrounds where drinking was taboo.

Almost all of us in our group, including Abdul Kalam, were vegetarians. In 1963 in this fairly remote little launching station in the heartland of USA, vegetarians like us were fairly unknown. And our staunch vegetarianism got us into some strange situations.

We were friends with a group of engineers and scientists from Italy who were training to set up a sea platform-based launcher called the San Marco platform off the coast near Venice. They wanted to launch NASA Scout rockets from there. Their proposal was to launch small satellites into low earth orbit (600–800 kms above the earth). Using this technique, they hoped to solve major range safety issues and create a versatile launch platform. The Italians were a group of jolly young men. Whenever they saw us carefully selecting vegetarian fare in the cafeteria they would taunt us as weaklings. If we lived on such food, they said, not just us, but even our women would become weak and they would never be able to bear strong babies!

Meanwhile, we were also befriended by some American employees who were members of a church group. They kept inviting us to attend one of their community gatherings. One fine day we decided to go. In the beginning they talked to us about Christianity, which we had expected. What followed, however, was amusing and at the same time a trifle disconcerting.

The meeting was followed by dinner and to our dismay we found there was nothing much we could eat. One of the leaders of the group walked up to us and urged us to eat meat because it would be sinful not to do so. He even quoted a passage from the Bible to prove his point. He said God had created man and ordered him to 'Be fruitful, and multiply, and replenish the earth, and subdue it.' Man had been created, he said, 'to have dominion over the fish of the sea, and over the fowl of the air, and over every living thing that moveth upon the earth'.

We were taken aback by the fervour of his words, but remained unmoved in our decision to remain vegetarian! Finally, our self-appointed mentor chided us, lifted his hands in prayer and said, 'Father forgive them for they know not what they do'! This experience taught us a lesson. We learned to avoid all invitations to join community dinners after that!

But we also left our own little vegetarian mark on the Wallops Island community before we departed. One day, when we were desperately looking around for some small eating place that could offer us a change from the monotonous fare at the cafeteria, we stumbled upon a home-based cafe run by a sweet old lady. She was puzzled when we asked for something vegetarian. She didn't really know what we wanted, but she made us an offer: we could use her kitchen and make ourselves whatever we wanted with the ingredients we found there, she said, and we could pay for it.

It seemed like a good deal. So we walked into her little kitchen and started piling everything vegetarian that we could find into a baking dish. Soon we had rice, vegetables, baked beans, onions, garlic, a few green peppers all mixed up together. We covered our dish with plenty of cheese and got the old lady to pop it into her oven. This hotchpotch dish turned out to be manna to our deadened taste buds! The old lady was very pleased too and whenever she saw us walking in she would start off our special dish which she had named the 'Thing'! We learned later that the dish became a local hit and that even Americans at Wallops would ask our old lady for the Indian 'Thing'!

During the latter part of our stay in Wallops, a group from Pakistan arrived there for training. In those days the Americans were even-handed when it came to India and Pakistan. If we built a sounding rocket range, so would Pakistan and NASA would provide similar assistance to them. The Pakistani team was a little larger in number and essentially had people similar to us in qualifications and experience. This was before the formation of Bangladesh so there were engineers from West as well as East Pakistan. We were rather wary of each other and carefully avoided talking politics.

Pakistan was also in the process of setting up a sounding rocket station similar to Thumba at a place called Sonmiani Beach near Karachi and they had a similar launch programme lined up. Looking back, I realize what a difference it made to have a visionary as our leader. Without Sarabhai India's space programme might have ended in the same doldrums as Pakistan's.

The Americans were aware, of course, of the Indo–Pak standoff and they had been told to be careful not to let our paths cross too closely. But since we were all housed in the same hostel we did have many friendly conversations. There were a few veterans who had lived in pre-Partition India and had fond memories of various Indian cities where they had been posted. We soon found that they were no different from us in attitude, culture or even language. We got on particularly well with our counterparts from East Pakistan (now Bangladesh) who seemed at that time to be more Indian in temperament than their West Pakistani colleagues.

The nearest town to Wallops was a place called Pocomoke City. On weekends we could request the range authorities to put a chauffeur-driven car at our disposal and we would spend the day shopping and looking around, although the town itself was pretty small.

We had another exciting 'perk'. NASA used to run a Dakota shuttle plane between Wallops and Washington, DC, via Langley where there was one more NASA centre. Langley was also the CIA headquarters. We were allowed to travel free of cost on this flight. So we would spend some weekends in DC where we stayed in some special hotels which charged only $6 per night if we showed our NASA ID cards. We could return to Wallops by the Monday morning shuttle plane well in time for our workday.

By the time we moved to Wallops we had mastered the operation of the telemetry receiving station. The focus now shifted to training us in radar tracking. We were positioned in a mobile radar unit called MPS 19. Soon we learned to operate it to track all kinds of rockets launched from the Wallops rocket range. We also practised tracking a variety of aircraft which flew around.

This radar, the telemetry and Doppler ground stations which were trailer mounted were all eventually shipped to Thumba in 1964. These systems continued to remain the property of NASA and were returned to them several years later. However, by the time they were returned to NASA, the technology had become obsolete and they were probably consigned to the scrap heap!

Meanwhile Kalam and Das learned how to assemble, transport, store and fire rockets. They were also taught about safety. In the early days, watching them go through mock firing exercises and countdown and hold sequences was a great source of amusement for all of us. Often Kalam and Das would miss the countdown sequence and press the red button either too early or too late. But they soon mastered the operation. And all of us became experts in the communication and intercom jargon of the range crew.

Meanwhile, back in India, some civil engineers led by R.D. John had started work on building the sounding rocket range in Trivandrum. By mid-1963 the basic range started taking shape. We started coordinating with them and providing details of the range, the safety distances, building plans, electrical details and so on. Towards the end of 1963, while we were at the final stages of our training, the preparations for the first launch from Thumba were at their peak. The Nike-Apache rocket provided by NASA and the sodium vapour payload package had been flown to Trivandrum. These were hazardous items and even their transportation from the US was a pioneering effort.

On 21 November 1963, India successfully launched its first sounding rocket. Easwaradas assembled the rocket and arranged the launch while Kalam was in charge of safety. Later, Abdul Kalam, who became one of my closest friends, told me of the problems they faced before they put the rocket on the launch pad.

The rocket was assembled in a church building acquired from the local fishing community. It was then shifted by a hydraulic crane to the launch pad. Apparently just as the rocket was about to be placed on the launch pad it started tilting because there was some leak in the hydraulic system. Luckily the rocket men on the spot were all young and strong, and they managed to physically hold the rocket and place it correctly on the launcher!

The sodium vapour cloud experiment was an interesting one. The payload of that first rocket consisted of a canister of sodium in the form of pellets. The scientists who had assembled this payload wanted to determine the properties of the upper atmospheric winds up to a height of about 200 km. The canister was ignited by an electronic timer at about 20 to 30 km during the rocket's vertical flight. Once it was ignited it released sodium vapour as it proceeded upwards, somewhat like a steam engine.

So, a vertical line of vapour was formed from about 30 km to about 200 km to begin with. And then, because of the varying winds at different heights, this line assumed the form of a constantly changing squiggle. Fixed cameras set up at three ground locations at known distances kept recording this varying pattern at synchronized intervals and at predetermined times. The only complication was that the vapour trail would be visible only if the sunlight directly illuminated it at a time when the background was already dark. Therefore we had to launch the rocket at twilight periods – either before sunrise or after sunset.

After the launch the scientists developed the pictures and calculated the properties of the upper winds at various heights. The term wind velocity at these heights means something totally different from winds at lower heights since the atmospheric density is so low that it is almost a vacuum. This vertical profiling was possible only with sounding rockets and not through satellites or ground measurements since it had to be done in situ.

Sometimes other chemicals and metallic elements like barium, lithium and trimethylaluminum were used for various scientific studies. These emitted different coloured vapours and provided dramatic visual displays to lay observers over large distances. The first orange vapour trail was visible from all over Kerala and parts of Tamil Nadu. This created great excitement since no one had ever seen such a sight. In fact, the Kerala Legislative Assembly, which was in session then, apparently adjourned temporarily to have a good view of the bright vapour trail in the western sky! There were also some news reports of 'weird sightings' which some reporters claimed were 'end of the world' omens!

NASA personnel who had gone to Thumba for the launch came back with glowing descriptions of the beautiful

Thumba beach dotted with coconut trees. They also narrated some apocryphal stories about how they launched the Nike-Apache using bullock carts for transportation and their own pocketknives for tools!

We were nearing the end of our training in radar tracking at the Wallops station and were preparing to pack up and head back home. Since the first launch carried no telemetry instrumentation and did not require radar tracking, our tracking expertise was not needed. But we had to get back before the launches began in earnest.

We at Wallops came to know of the launch only the next day: we were thrilled when the announcement about India's successful launch was made on the Wallops Island intercom. Our NASA colleagues congratulated us. Soon after that, we went back to packing up our equipment. And then we heard another announcement on the intercom.

'We regret to announce that our beloved President Kennedy has been shot dead in Dallas…'

There was a shocked silence. Everyone in the range seemed to fall silent for a moment. But, what surprised me most was that after the brief pause, work went on as if nothing had happened! There was no break in work, no government declaration of a holiday or a day of mourning as we would have had in India.

Over the next few days, we were glued to the black-and-white TV sets looking for news. And news we had in plenty! We saw Kennedy's body being flown to Washington, DC, and the Vice President Lyndon Johnson being sworn in as President right on Air Force One as Mrs Kennedy was watching the funeral procession. Our hearts melted as we watched Kennedy's small son walking valiantly in front of the procession. In subsequent days we saw the drama unfold further with the arrest and almost immediate assassination of Lee Harvey Oswald, the alleged assassin of Kennedy, right in front of the TV cameras. The man who killed Oswald was himself killed, thus creating a super mystery, which to this day has never been fully solved.

But for us, it was back to work. Also, Buddy and I were really looking forward to going back home. After packing and dispatching the NASA instrumentation trailers, we left the US, taking different routes. I stopped over at London, Paris and Rome, and reached Bombay where I reported to DAE. I was then formally transferred to Thumba.

Then it was back to Madras, home sweet home.

I come from a family of nine. My parents and some of my siblings were eagerly waiting for me. After all, I was the very first foreign returnee in our family. I regaled them with tales of my American sojourn and distributed the gifts I had brought. I had bought a Yashica camera, and for the first time I got my large extended family of parents, siblings and assorted relatives to pose for pictures together.

At the tail end of December 1963, I finally caught a train to Trivandrum. I was once again received by Ramakrishna Rao, this time at the Trivandrum railway station – a place that was going to become a second home over the next couple of years! He took me to a nearby lodge where I was to stay for the time being. I reported at Thumba the next day.

2
Those Were the Days

I was born in south India and had lived there for the first twenty-two years of my life, but I had never visited Kerala. My first glimpse of Kerala from the train was breathtaking. Miles and miles of intense green, picturesque beaches and beautiful flowing rivers... I felt I had entered some sort of a paradise.

But the reality of my situation hit me very soon. I was a big city boy – first living in Madras, then Bombay and finally Washington, DC. It took me just a few days to understand that the contrast between those places and Trivandrum was quite stark.

Although Trivandrum was the state capital, it was a sleepy, slow town with old tiled houses lost amidst coconut groves. The roads were narrow and curvy with sharp turns and fast-changing slopes. There were acres of rice fields right in the heart of the city. Trivandrum seemed like an overgrown village. All the people were dressed very conservatively, with both the men and women wearing the white Kerala mundu.

The day after I arrived, I caught the only means of transport to Thumba: a rattling state transport bus which started from near the railway station and reached the rocket range by a long and circuitous route. It took me more than one hour to cover 20 km even in those zero traffic days! Our bus wound its way through what seemed to be an endless, serpentine avenue lined with coconut trees interspersed with mud-walled thatched huts. The intensity of the greenery was overwhelming. There were some houses with tiled roofs as well, but no grand buildings like in Madras. Unlike in other parts of the country, there was no clearly defined city or group of villages separated by empty spaces. Human habitations stretched in one long line. And it all seemed to blend harmoniously with the natural environment.

Kesavadasapuram, Ulloor, Kulathoor, Kazhakkuttam and Pallithura... Although my mother tongue was Tamil which seemed phonetically similar to Malayalam, I found these tongue-twisting names difficult to remember. Over the years they became very familiar, of course, but on that first bus ride everything, including the place names, seemed quite exotic.

As we rattled along I tried to remember all the information I had about Thumba. This site was chosen because it was ideally situated beneath the magnetic equator and comparatively less populated. Although some other beaches were also surveyed, Thumba seemed ideal because it was close to Trivandrum, the state capital, and all the essential logistics including air, rail and road connectivity were in place.

A large tract of land, mostly beach, had been acquired from a local fishing community. The fishermen lived in thatched huts and the few permanent structures in the area were the church, the bishop's house and a school building. Everyone was talking about the genial collector Madhavan Nair who bonded easily with the fishermen. It was Nair who had managed to get this location for the launch station. The fisherfolk trusted him totally when he assured them that they would be rehabilitated on a nearby beach with better living conditions. Their local bishop was also convinced. And so they had already vacated their land and moved to Pallithura, a couple of miles away. DAE and the Kerala state government had collaborated with the bishop to construct a pleasant colony for them, complete with a new church.

I had to report to H.G.S. Murthy who had temporarily set up his office at the vacant bishop's house adjoining the now empty church building. Easwaradas and Abdul Kalam, who had already played a role in the first launch, were also in the bishop's house.

I was highly excited on my very first day. I took a bicycle and pedalled around the range. The new roads interconnecting the launch pad, blockhouse and other installations were already laid. The range had a coastal length of about 2 km and an area of about 600 acres, mostly covered with coconut and cashew trees. I met some of the staff who had been deputed there for the construction work, and the few technical people who had been maintaining the range systems. Everything was peaceful, as I had landed just between launches.

In those early days we had no canteen or even an eating place close by. We had to grab an early breakfast from the canteen at the railway station close to our lodge, buy some lunch from there and carry it along. There was not much work to be done and anyway the to-and-fro commute by the local bus took up most of our day.

The range was quite large in area and the only means of transport inside were bicycles. Some colleagues, like Kalam, who could not cycle, had to hitch rides with others. Sometimes rocket parts were carried on the pillion. For larger equipment we used a crane or even sometimes a bullock cart. There were no strict working hours and work went on around the clock.

The second launch was scheduled for early January 1964. Soon the range was abuzz with preparations. This too was a sodium vapour release launch and Professor P.D. Bhavsar was the project scientist in command. I assumed charge as the head of ground instrumentation. The radar and telemetry stations had not yet arrived from the US but this particular launch did not call for any such tracking. We only needed intercoms and radio communication and electronic timing.

Bhavsar had set up camera stations in three towns around Thumba: Palayamkottah, Quilon and Cape Comorin (now known as Kanyakumari). These stations needed to be in constant touch with the launch base in order to track the sodium cloud accurately. Those were the days of abysmal telephone connectivity and poor Bhavsar struggled to operate the telephone lines which were constantly 'down'. His was a tough task as he had to ensure clear weather in all stations as well as proper time synchronization for good photographic results.

Kalam was in charge of range safety, which covered land, sea and air, Easwaradas the rocket assembly chief, and H.G.S. Murthy was the overall test director. There was a small band of other technical personnel as part of the operations staff. The first rocket had been assembled in the church building, but by now the permanent assembly hall for the rockets and the storage bunkers had been commissioned.

The launch lift-off had to be either at dusk or dawn light because only then would the background be dark and the trail bright. Usually the countdown had to be carried out until the last moment. The launch was made only when all the camera stations had confirmed clear weather. Subsequently I took part in several launches where the crew had to work continuously on successive dawns and dusks until the skies cleared.

But on this, my very first launch from our own rocket station, we were lucky. We were able to launch on the first day itself and the cameras performed reasonably well. Although I had witnessed many Nike-Apache launchings from Wallops, it was altogether a different feeling to see the powerful blast-off and the vehicle taking off majestically from our own pad located amidst the green canopy.

The main area in which I had received training – telemetry and tracking – had not been exercised yet since the trailers housing these systems had not arrived from NASA. Meanwhile, the preparations for locating them, such as site clearance, power connection and communication, were being established. These systems were commissioned in late 1964 for payloads carrying telemetry.

One piece of equipment that gave us severe transportation challenges was a long trailer called the Doppler Velocity and Positioning System (DOVAP), built by NASA. This came to us as part of the initial collaborative agreement with NASA.

The DOVAP trailer arrived by ship, docking in the Madras harbour in mid-1964. This large container-like trailer was nearly 40 feet long and housed a ground station for tracking the flight path of sounding rockets. A self-contained unit, it had its own air-conditioning systems, electronic equipment and spares, and even had a couple of beds for resting during those long twenty-four hour workdays.

The DOVAP was to be cleared through customs at Madras, brought by road to Trivandrum without damage and installed at Thumba. In 1964 container trailers were a rarity in India and we did not have good roads or facilities for transporting them. But we had no choice – the trailer was lying in the Madras harbour and had to be transported to Trivandrum, a distance of about 800 km by road.

Since I was from Madras and familiar with the equipment, I was promptly dispatched to get the task done. Customs clearing was not a big issue since a government-to-government agreement had been signed. The handling and transportation of the mammoth trailer was the major task. I sought the advice of my father who had some experience in this kind of thing. He put me on to a contractor who was willing to take it on.

Everything was a learning experience for me. We had to find a special tractor and fabricate fixtures to attach it to the trailer. Then I had to configure the optimum route to Trivandrum without sharp bends and steep inclines so that the equipment could be safely driven to the destination without getting stuck midway.

The DOVAP had to pass on the highway in front of my father's house in Chromepet. On D-Day, all my brothers and sisters, their friends and other extended family members gathered to watch the vehicle as it rolled majestically by. Finally the equipment moved out of Madras along the Grand Trunk Road. It was very cautiously driven through the chosen route with a pilot car in front. All along the route the local police had to be kept informed. The movement of the DOVAP caused considerable excitement and local people gathered along the way to watch what they mistakenly thought was a giant rocket being transported!

Finally, the system reached Thumba and was positioned in the range for commissioning. All of us including the contractor heaved huge sighs of relief. Later, the contractor asked for more money to compensate for the stress he had faced! The DOVAP was used for a few launches, but mainly it provided a nice air-conditioned laboratory enclosure for other developmental work.

After that first buzz of activity we had a lull period during which I got acclimatized to my new routine. The first set of Nike-Apaches had already been launched. The next scheduled launches were a few months away. Everyone looked relaxed and at leisure. We had lots of spare time to walk along the beach and wet our feet in the waves. However, swimming was a strict no-no since the sea there was very rough and deep with dangerous currents. Occasionally we used to get someone to climb the nearest coconut tree and have refreshing coconut water. The permanent staff positioned at the range was hardly a handful and the atmosphere was more that of a family rather than a formal launch base.

Small changes occurred gradually. We hired a few cooks and set up a small canteen. Soon the range acquired a jeep in addition to a Standard van and these were pressed into round-the-clock duties. Our first bus arrived a few months later. Reaching the range became easier.

By the mid-1960s space scientists from all over the world started coming to conduct experiments with sounding rockets at Thumba. Those were simple times when there was an extraordinary amount of goodwill amongst the international community of scientists. For instance, as a gesture of that goodwill, Russia (or the USSR as it was known then) contributed a military helicopter for range safety and a computer called the Minsk. This was the only computer we had in those days.

The helicopter was actually a brandnew one. Rumour had it that the machine had been donated to us with just an informal wave of the hand from one of the all-powerful 'Academicians' as the senior scientists were called in Russia in those days. Did he want to give us a really good present as a gesture of goodwill or did he want to show off Russia's might to the Americans? It didn't matter! We were the beneficiaries. Imagine the red tape and complicated minefields we would have to circumnavigate today if we were to receive such a 'donation'! This machine was usually used for surveying the range and making sure the sea was clear of fishermen and boats and ships before we launched our sounding rockets.

I had an interesting personal experience with the Russian chopper. In the early 1960s we did not have a map of our range. Since TERLS was a restricted area, it was very difficult to even get permission to get a proper survey done. So Murthy hit upon a bright idea. He suggested I take my camera and fly over the range in the helicopter and take some pictures. We could piece them together and form our own survey map.

My Yashica camera, which I had bought in the US, was one of my most prized possessions. Since I was also a fairly good photographer, by then I had, willy-nilly, become Thumba's official photographer. I used to joke that the photography section was contained in the right-hand drawer of my tiny desk.

All of twenty-five, I was very excited by Murthy's suggestion. My close friend and lodge mate Abdul Kalam, who had a good camera as well, was assigned to come with me. The pilot was a retired IAF man who had been given some special training in handling the helicopter. Before we boarded the flight, he briefed us.

Since it was a military helicopter, the machine came with some special belts used by bombers to strap themselves to the floor. There was also a hatch on the floor, probably used for dropping bombs as well as food supplies. The captain told us we would be strapped to the floor of the helicopter and we could train our cameras through the hatch. He would decide which would be the correct position to take a picture. When he reached the spot he would hover over it. He would then use a horn placed next to him to give a loud honk because the rotor of the helicopter was so noisy we would not be able to hear him talk. We would then have to take the photos.

It was an exciting, unforgettable ride. We got breathtaking panoramic views of our range through the sides of the chopper. We held our cameras steady, pointed them through the hatch and took what we thought were excellent pictures.

But, sadly, the photos we took proved to be totally useless! Those were the days before zoom lenses and the beauty and details of the range which stretched below us simply could not be captured with our amateur cameras. We had to wait several more years before we could get our range properly mapped.

Back on land, we got busy as the frequency of our launches increased. Since there were very few concrete buildings, the church of Mary Magdalene around which all our initial activity was centred continued to be a focal point. This church had an interesting history. Like many other ancient churches in this part of the world, this one too could trace its roots back to the sixteenth century when St Francis Xavier came to Kerala. St Francis was a zealous missionary who was responsible for converting to Christianity many of the fishing communities living along the coast. Legend has it that he built the first structure – a prayer hall with mud walls and a roof made of coconut frond thatch. This structure apparently lasted nearly a hundred years until the Jesuits replaced it with a church dedicated to St Bartholomew.

The present church came into existence at the turn of the twentieth century. In its new avatar it became the church of Mary Magdalene when the fishermen who were building the structure found a beautiful sandalwood statue of the saint lying on the beach. This statue was consecrated and placed on the altar of the new church. An unusually long log of wood that had drifted in from the sea was erected as the flag post and the church became functional.

When we took it over, the church building, as we called it, was one of the few brick and mortar structures in the area. Although it was a modest-sized church, it had a special aura. It had ceased to be a place of worship, but for us pioneers at ISRO it was a very special hub where some of our most exciting projects were conceived.

Its high-raftered roof was a sanctuary to swarms of pigeons. The altar in front of the statue of Mary Magdalene was left untouched as we had promised the fisherfolk that this sacred area would be preserved as it was. And many of the early rockets, including the very first Nike-Apache, were assembled in front of the altar. The central portion of the church became a bustling office space. Later, assemblies took place in the newly built rocket assembly hall. Once that move occurred, the various wings of the church were used to provide temporary accommodation to the scientists and the support staff.

By the mid-sixties, plans were afoot to start a space science and technology centre in the picturesque Veli Hills close by. A couple of scientists working in foreign universities and laboratories had already been recruited so that they could start planning the future programmes. Many of them had PhDs from prestigious foreign universities and they arrived in Trivandrum bag and baggage, families in tow, directly from abroad.

And so, the church building came in handy once more! The main assembly wing of the church was partitioned into cubicles. The newly arrived scientists sat in these makeshift offices and went to work on the preliminary planning and recruitment of staff. We had the basic facilities in place now, but we all had to live with the flocks of pigeons and their offspring!

Visitors, especially other scientists coming from abroad, were often taken aback by this strange sight. Many of them made appreciative noises about the innovative spirit of Indians and lauded our passion for and determination to enter the space age despite the hurdles. But for us, these were not hurdles – we were doing exciting things and over the years the church had become our home and the pigeons our family.

As the years rolled by and more structures came up, the church building served as a general-purpose covered space that could be used as a stop-gap area. Finally this iconic building was converted into a modern space museum with audiovisual presentations and models. Today, it attracts hordes of school children and many visitors who love the special conducted tours of the museum.

We also had a number of old but usable brick structures scattered across the range. For a long time these served as office spaces for various sections such as the construction division, the security division and the canteen. The bishop's residence adjoining the church was the office of the test director of TERLS and some senior engineers until the control centre was built. A small primary school building close to the launch pad temporarily served as a launch office and was subsequently converted into a technical library.

All the buildings were hardly a few metres away from the seashore which was dotted with hundreds of coconut trees. I could walk out of my office right on to the beach for some fresh air whenever I wanted. The fishermen continued to claim the beach as their natural fishing zone and their nets lay on the sands. They would fish and move across the beach, clearing the area just a few hours before a launch.

My office area evolved as the activities on the range increased. My very first workspace was in the bishop's house. After that I moved into the school building and then into one of the cubicles in the church. Finally, when the control centre on the beach was completed I had my own office there. It was just a small room but I had a PA and my own desk.

3

TERLS: The International Launch Station

During the 1960s, TERLS was an international launch station. Our doors were open to everyone. In those initial days rigid security systems were not in place, and a most eclectic collection of visitors walked in and out of our range. It was during this period that the famous French photographer Henri Cartier-Bresson visited TERLS.

Cartier-Bresson came to India in 1966. He had made a visit to Gujarat on that trip and Sarabhai, who was a personal friend, invited him to Thumba. He had visited India before. His photographs of the heady pre-Independence days and the stunning pictures of Gandhiji's funeral were famous the world over. But at that point of time, we at Thumba were just a bunch of young kids, blissfully unaware of his fame.

Cartier-Bresson must have been in his mid-fifties then. All I remember of him was that he was a tall, balding Frenchman who spoke with a strong accent. He was usually dressed in a bush shirt and trousers and wore a vest with several pockets in which he would have stuffed rolls of film. He also carried a well-used brown cloth bag. With minimal security on the range, Cartier-Bresson, like many others of our foreign visiting scientists, had a free run of the place. He could just wander around and choose his subjects and the timing of his shots.

Although I had no official role in his visit, I had a lot of time and opportunity to watch him at work. I was absolutely fascinated by the way he would unobtrusively lurk around in the background and click away with his rather simple cameras loaded with black and white rolls.

Much later when I knew who he really was, I read up about him and learned that he took some of his most unforgettable shots in this manner. Apparently he always only used a Leica rangefinder and a single lens, which allowed him to focus his attention on his subject without using a viewfinder. He would also wrap his camera in black to make it unobtrusive so he could just walk up to his subject and shoot without being noticed. He did not believe in using the flash, which he considered intrusive, and disliked colour photography which he had tried a couple of times.

I personally featured in two classic shots taken by him. The first was taken on a sweltering day in Trivandrum. Kalam and I were fixing a timer unit to a sodium vapour cloud payload. Those were still our makeshift days and we were both crouched on the floor of the church building in front of the altar. We had no fans, let alone air conditioning. It was so unbearably hot that I had removed my shirt. Both of us were intently focused on what we were doing. Kalam was getting more and more anxious as the wretched payload unit would not sit properly and we were running out of time. Neither of us bothered about the old man with the camera who had wandered in and was busy capturing our anxious moments!

Little did we realize then that we would be featured in what was to become an iconic shot. Although this picture was used in many of the brochures produced by ISRO in later years, it became really famous only after it went viral on the internet soon after Kalam became the President of India. Since both of us were very young in that picture most of the viewers who did not know us were confused as to who was who. And for the record, I was the shirtless guy fixing the unit and Kalam was the anxious guy looking on!

The second shot by Cartier-Bresson caught me in another fraught moment. The rocket was already on the launch pad and the countdown was held up because something had gone wrong with the high-speed camera. This piece of equipment was absolutely essential for the launch and I was working against time to fix it. Bresson caught that frantic look on my face as I peered into the misbehaving camera. This classic picture featured in a small brochure of Cartier-Bresson's best pictures of TERLS brought out by Professor Bhavsar.

Two more characteristic pictures he took also went viral later. One showed my colleague and friend C.R. Sathya cycling along with a rocket nose cone on his carrier. The other was a shot of a group of school children looking up at the rocket take-off, their faces etched with a mix of thrill and fear. This was taken near the church building and they were probably watching the takeoff of the American meteorological rocket called the Skua. The launch pad for this particular rocket was close to the church building.

And I also have a private and personal image of Cartier-Bresson. One day when I was walking across the beach from one building to another, I saw him lying flat under a coconut palm, his camera pointed upwards. I don't really know what shot he was trying to frame, but that image of him, in particular, has stayed with me forever.

Cartier-Bresson was just one of the many foreigners who visited TERLS in the 1960s. The range was being developed as a facility to provide a launch location to scientists from all over the world who were interested in studying the equatorial electro jet. It was encouraged and supported by many western countries including the US, USSR, France, UK and West Germany. There was no monetary contribution by other countries, but they gave us range equipment like telemetry receivers, tracking systems and computers. Some of them came on loan and some were outright gifts.

India for its part offered to dedicate the facility to the United Nations as a goodwill gesture. The UN also formally sponsored TERLS as an international scientific facility open to all its members. There were no financial commitments on either side. In 1968, TERLS was formally dedicated to the UN by the then prime minister, Indira Gandhi. Subsequently, the UN named an advisory panel consisting of eminent scientists from various countries to suggest scientific programmes of relevance that could be carried out at TERLS. This panel, which met regularly in Thumba or New York, would review the work done and chalk out future plans.

Thumba had many programmes under collaboration with a variety of Indian and foreign agencies. We also used a range of rockets including Centaures, Nike-Apaches, Dragons, Skuas, Judi-Darts, Arcas, RH-300s and RH-200s.

'We are like a giant studio set,' H.G.S. Murthy, our range director, would often say, as scientists from across the world trooped into TERLS, launched their rockets and left. 'We provide the location and the equipment. But they are the main actors!' Sometimes the scientists brought their own equipment and at other times they used ours. But at almost all times we were just the guys who provided technical help with the launch; we often had nothing to do with the experiments or with analysing the data.

Sometimes, when Murthy got fed up with unreasonable demands from the visiting scientists, he would grumble, 'One of these days some scientist is going to come and ask me to launch a rocket with a packet of halwa – and I will do it too!'

The earliest foreign scientists who came to Thumba were from the US and France. They came to conduct vapour cloud experiments. The Americans helped set up some of the facilities at Thumba and provided training to the initial set of Indian technicians. They also gave us our first set of Nike-Apache rockets; these were used to carry the scientific payloads that their scientists launched from Thumba under a collaborative agreement with us. Officials from the NASA headquarters, such as Arnold Fruitkin of the international cooperation division, visited us during the initial days. Sarabhai and some other members of his team made reciprocal visits to NASA to finalize the details. However, the working level teams were always present at TERLS for the actual launch missions.

During the first launch, for which I was not present, there was a team of rocket assembly and launch technicians who were flown down from the US especially for this mission. When they returned to NASA they told their bosses that they had to work under the most primitive conditions. But the launches were mostly successful and they went back with their data.

The second set of launches, which involved telemetry and Doppler tracking, had a much larger team in place. Senior engineers from the sounding rocket division of NASA came to Thumba for commissioning the ground stations which were essential for these launches. Karl Medrow, the division chief, was there and so was Ed Bissell, the actual man in charge. Bissell had been our training coordinator at NASA and so we were able to work easily with him.

The facilities and infrastructure at Thumba being quite basic, the visitors initially found it strange and tough to work under these conditions. They came from a much more sophisticated environment where they could take so many things for granted. Here, even though they mostly brought their own tools, they still often found the local support system inadequate. They were especially bothered by the frequent power outages and fluctuations. Soon we got things a little more streamlined. We started providing captive generators for the actual launches. Our team of engineers and technicians grew, and we also became more experienced in handling problems.

The foreign scientists had to stay in Mascot Hotel in the centre of Trivandrum, the only hotel in the city that provided them with somewhat acceptable accommodation. Most of them were quite conservative in their food habits and would commute back to the hotel even for their meals. But what all of them enjoyed was the exotic change that the visit to India offered them. They were happy to take a break from their grey skies and dreary routine back home. They would have left their cold western countries during winter, and the tropical weather and clear skies at Thumba located on the beach lined with coconut palms offered them a paradise-like environment.

Soon there was a steady stream of foreign scientists visiting Thumba for discussions as well as launch campaigns. We even had an international seminar organized by Sarabhai at Thumba. It was held in one of the abandoned primary school buildings on the beach and our 'conference hall' was nothing but a shed slightly spruced up for the occasion.

Gathering in such basic environs, scientists from the US, USSR, France, Britain and some other countries forgot their political affiliations and held intense discussions on how the range could be effectively used for atmospheric research under the overall umbrella of the UN. Quite a few collaborative programmes were initiated in that forum. These later matured into important campaigns. How different it was from the air-conditioned halls with plush seats and state-of-the-art audio and video equipment we use for seminars these days!

My one and only close encounter with Homi Bhabha happened at Thumba in late 1964, hardly a year before his tragic death. I had only once before seen the great man from a distance when I was a rookie engineer at DAE. I had never thought I would one day actually speak to him! I was busy inside the telemetry receiving trailer when I heard a knock. I looked up and to my shock saw Sarabhai walking in with Homi Bhabha himself!

'Homi, you know Aravamudan. He is one of your boys from the reactor control division,' Sarabhai said. 'He has just returned from NASA and is a specialist in telemetry and tracking.'

Bhabha gave me one of his rare smiles and warmly shook my hand. Maybe he was proud of me for having joined Thumba, I thought hopefully, as I stood there frozen with excitement.

'Dan, tell Dr Bhabha about your work,' Sarabhai said with an encouraging nod.

I shook myself out of my trance and started explaining the workings of the telemetry system. He asked a few searching questions, shook my hand again and left. Later at lunch he talked to all of us about our future work. It was a brief encounter but one that I still cherish. A little later in January 1966, we got the shocking news of his death in the Air India plane crash over the Alps.

In those early days whenever we had visitors in between the launches, there was nothing very dramatic to show them on the range. Usually my telemetry and radar trailers became the showpieces, and every visitor would be packed off for a demonstration and explanation. Soon I had a set routine. I would explain the workings, put on a tape recording of an actual launch taking place in NASA, and then rotate the radar and telemetry equipment for them to see.

One day Kakkan, a minister from Tamil Nadu, came to visit our range. Those were very early days and we had just our school building and a launch pad. Since I spoke Tamil I took him around and explained everything to him. He was a very humble and polite man who even insisted on personally disposing of the coconut husk after he finished his drink of fresh coconut water.

At the end of my conducted tour he suddenly turned around and asked me, 'Thambi, how many people have you sent up in your rockets so far?' I was dumbstruck – so much for my explanations in pure, perfect Tamil!

Another day we had a glamorous visitor who turned up unannounced. One of our Malayali engineers who was cycling past the radar trailer spotted a safari suit-clad gentleman sporting sunshades standing alone and looking around. Our engineer almost fell down with excitement. It was the legendary Prem Nazir himself!

'Nazir sir,' he gasped.

Nazir removed his shades and gave him a broad smile. 'I heard our Malayali boys were launching rockets here,' he said. 'I was passing by on my way to a shooting and thought I would look in.'

By then quite an excited crowd had gathered. We all escorted him to the school building where everything was explained to him in Malayalam. He saw the launch pad and left, promising to come again to see a launch.

On another hot day, when I was sitting in the school building, I got a call from one of the security men. A person who claimed to be an MP from Kerala was attempting to get in, he said. He had no identity card or pass. I told him to escort the gentleman to my room.

The MP was seething by the time he came. He refused to have a guided tour or even a drink of tender coconut water. 'Give me some paper,' he said. 'I need to write a note to Vikram'.

I had no option but to give him the paper.

'Dear Vikram,' he wrote. 'Please instruct your people to treat MPs more politely.'

He gave me the note and said, 'It's nothing personal. Just see that it reaches him.' And he left.

That was the last I heard from him. I told Sarabhai about this incident on his next visit. He just smiled and made no comment.

When the Dalai Lama visited Thumba in the early 1960s he was still in his twenties – almost the same age as me. He had not yet learned to speak English and had to use an interpreter. As usual I explained to him the workings of the telemetry system and described the rocket flight. He was palpably excited. He wanted to learn a lot more about rocketry, he said through his interpreter. Finally, when he was about to leave, he put his arm around me and gave me his trademark wide smile. I felt a great sense of bonding with this man whom I never met again.

J.R.D. Tata also visited us. The moment he stepped into the trailer, it was obvious to me that he belonged to a different world. His dashing looks and flamboyant language flustered me somewhat. However, I managed to go through my by now well-rehearsed explanation. And finally I played the launch tape for him. The countdown was over and we heard the rocket take off.

'Good! The damn thing took off on the dot,' he remarked as he turned around and left. I was in a state of shock. That was the first time I had heard our precious rockets being referred to as 'damn' things!

In 1968, Indira Gandhi, who became the prime minister of India in 1966, came to Thumba to dedicate TERLS to the UN. As usual I had to take her to the telemetry trailer and explain the system to her. As I was earnestly explaining telemetry to her, I was disconcerted to see Mrs Gandhi's gaze fixed steadily on the top of my head. I was worried. She was after all the prime minister of India. Why was she looking at the top of my head instead of listening to me? Was I that boring or obscure? As soon as I finished she asked me her first question, with a serious expression, 'Did NASA measure your height before building this trailer?'

Seeing my stunned look, she burst out laughing and pointed to the top of my head. I am 6 feet 2 inches tall, and since it was the trailer had a low ceiling, my head was brushing the top. I had to be careful not to bump my head when I stood inside. As I smiled bashfully and touched the top of my head, I wondered whether she had actually listened to any of my technical explanations!

One day I had two cute little visitors who listened to every bit of my explanation with utmost interest. Sarabhai had come on an unusual visit with his daughter Mallika and son Kartikeya. It was a beautiful sunny day and the two pre-teen kids were playing on the beach in front of the church. I remember Mallika was dressed in a traditional south Indian skirt and blouse.

Suddenly Sarabhai called me and said, 'Dan, if you don't mind could you take these two and show them your tracking systems.'

I took them to a radar trailer parked close by. They listened very closely to my explanation and even asked me some questions. I wondered then whether they too would grow up to be scientists like their father.

A rather interesting person with whom we had plenty of contact in those initial days was Professor Hideo Itokawa from the University of Tokyo. He was a short man with a good sense of humour. In Japan he was known as Dr Rocket – he had led the development of rocket technology in Japan from scratch. In the 1950s he designed and flew tiny rockets to understand the various parameters of a rocket flight. He experimented in university laboratories with his small models before going on to build sounding rockets and bigger vehicles.

Sarabhai was obviously impressed by his work and enthusiasm. He roped him in as a consultant while setting up the Space Science and Technology Centre (SSTC) on

Veli Hills in Thumba. He also asked the professor to help him with recruiting Indian scientists who were working abroad. The professor jumped into the task with his usual enthusiasm. He wrote later about the challenges he faced during this time in his book *The Third Road: India, Japan and Entropy.*

'To start a new laboratory there was literally nothing: no funds, no human resources, no organization, no building and no facilities! In fact it was a start from zero!' he wrote. He found that many qualified engineers and scientists who had studied in foreign universities were reluctant to return home to India. 'This was not just brain drain but Indian brain living abroad! We put our advertisement in foreign newspapers and journals: "Wanted. Qualified personnel in science, computer engineering etc. for the newly established Space Science Research Laboratory. Salary negotiable."'

Sarabhai, however, did manage to persuade some bright and experienced scientists and engineers to return home. How much of this was due to the professor's efforts is still a matter of speculation. His interaction with the space programme was only for a short period but he left an impact on the way we approached problems. He taught us to innovate, to learn from our own mistakes and to work as a team towards a predetermined goal. We were still learning to take our baby steps when he arrived on the scene. He would constantly remind us that rocket technology was a closely guarded secret and the only way to master it was by trial and error.

As SSTC evolved in later years Professor Itokawa's association with ISRO tapered off. I came to know that, sadly, he got into trouble with the Japanese government over some issues and became persona non grata there. Nearly a decade later, during a visit to Tokyo my colleagues and I tried to meet him, but he was reluctant to see us.

4

Finding Our Feet – and Wings

In the early 1960s the goal of India's rocket pioneers was pretty simple: they wanted to establish a modest sounding rocket launching facility at Thumba. Sarabhai had prepared a ten-year blueprint which envisioned creating indigenous satellites and rocket launchers but this was properly articulated only by the mid-1960s. That was when we started acquiring land for more buildings and facilities.

The buildings that came up initially were around Veli Hills. These were the Space Science and Technology Centre (SSTC), the Rocket Propellant Plant (RPP) and the Rocket Fabrication Facility (RFF). Soon, the cluster of buildings in the area began to grow. Meanwhile, Sarabhai started looking for an area on the eastern coast to establish a launch station for bigger rockets which could launch satellites, both low earth orbit ones and geosynchronous ones, into space.

By the mid-1960s, an active recruitment drive started. Whenever Sarabhai went abroad, he would meet scientists and engineers working in the area of space technology and describe to them his vision of the Indian space programme. With his charisma and visionary descriptions of the future, he drew some of the most qualified engineers and scientists back to India. Some of them were working in well-established space agencies like NASA, but they were excited at the idea of being part of this nascent space programme in their homeland.

The main thrust, however, was to get as many recruits as possible from our own homegrown universities. Soon I became part of the recruiting team and am proud to say I had the opportunity to pull into the team some very bright young men and women who rose to great heights within the organization.

Around 1967, since Thumba was still part of DAE, Sarabhai decided the latter was the obvious place to look for recruits. The DAE training school was a highly sought-after institution in those days. It used to churn out about 150 to 200 young scientists and engineers, all of whom had been selected at an all-India level after careful screening. Since I was an old DAE hand myself, Sarabhai asked me to attend a meeting of the placement panel and make sure that at least a few of the successful trainees were allotted to Thumba. He felt that those hailing from south India and Kerala in particular might like to join the space programme.

The demand for staff from the mainstream DAE was so high that initially I was very doubtful whether we would get any candidate at all. But I got help from unexpected quarters. The chairman of the panel was Dr Brahm Prakash, director of the chemical and metallurgy Group of DAE. He overruled other voices and decided to allot three candidates to Thumba.

When I emerged from the meeting room, I found a big gathering of trainees eagerly waiting to find out more about where they would be working and what they would be doing. Understandably, most of the candidates wanted to be posted in the major centres of DAE and they were not interested in coming down south, especially to a unit whose future was uncertain.

I had to attract some attention. I am a tall man and I decided to use my height! I stood up and, pulling myself as straight as I could, raised my hands above my head and started calling out: 'Thumba! Trivandrum!'

After a while, three candidates approached me. Two of them, G. Madhavan Nair, an electronics engineer, and N.R.U.K. Kartha, a mechanical engineer, were from Trivandrum, while Rangarajan was an electronics engineer from IIT Madras. They were unsure as to whether they should continue with DAE or venture down south to a relatively unknown organization. I had to paint an appealing picture of what was in store.

I told them that one day India would be an important player in the field of rocketry, and if they joined now, they would be pioneers in this exciting new venture. The scope of our activities was quite limited in those days and we had not even started talking about satellite launch vehicles and satellites, but I didn't tell them that! They decided to join. The rest is history. Madhavan Nair had the most spectacular rise of the three and ended up as chairman of ISRO.

I could empathize with the young recruits because I myself had faced this dilemma a couple of times. The first time was when I took that decision to leave my cushy job at DAE and plunge into this totally unknown and untested field. Raja Ramanna's words still rang in my ears.

The second time was when I went to meet a senior IAS officer in Bombay to get some papers signed. He spoke to me for a while and asked about my background. Then, with a sigh, he picked up the papers. 'I don't know why you gave up a good government job and got hooked into this hare-brained scheme,' he said. 'Maybe you should reconsider. You can always go back to your old job.' Many years later he became a very integral part of the administration in ISRO, but he was such a formidable gentleman that I didn't want to remind him of his sceptical comment which I had fortunately taken with a pinch of salt!

The third time I had a moment of doubt was when I received an official letter saying I would have to opt either to stay in DAE and continue to be a government employee or go into Sarabhai's project and become an employee of PRL, which was a non-governmental organization. Worried, I even wrote to PRL, asking what would happen to my central government perks including my Provident Fund if I opted for PRL. Their response was not very clear. But this whole field was so exciting and I knew all along that this was the job for me, so I decided to stay. In the long run I did lose out a couple of years of service because I had moved from one organization to another, but I never had any regrets.

In the early 1960s, the average age of our little organization was around twenty-seven years. Amazingly, a few years later the average age dropped as we recruited more and more raw young graduates. By the time I was thirty, I was one of the most senior employees of our space research team!

The early scientists and engineers came from disparate streams. The PRL at Ahmedabad was Sarabhai's 'mother' organization. It was here that the planning of the space science and technology activity in India took place. Many of his recruits came from there. There were also the young recruits from DAE and the slightly more experienced engineers from other related organizations. And finally there were the scientists and engineers of Indian origin whom Sarabhai had picked up from foreign universities and organizations.

Most of the recruits from PRL had studied atmospheric physics under Sarabhai. E.V. Chitnis, P.D. Bhavsar and S.R. Thakore were the very early recruits from PRL who now continued to work in the space programme. Chitnis was the soft-spoken Maharashtrian I had met on my very first trip to Ahmedabad. He was a student of Sarabhai's and had worked on cosmic rays as part of his PhD programme at the Massachusetts Institute of Technology (MIT). However, after a three-year stay at MIT he had returned home to become a member of the PRL faculty. In 1961 Chitnis set up the Satellite Telemetry Station at PRL. When the Indian National Committee for Space Research (INCOSPAR) – which would become ISRO in 1969 – was constituted in 1962, he became its member-secretary. From then on, he was very closely involved with all aspects of the space

programme, including the establishment of TERLS and
SSTC in Trivandrum and the setting up of the Experimental
Satellite Communication Earth Station (which became part
of the Space Applications Centre) at Ahmedabad. Chitnis
was virtually Sarabhai's second-in-command.

Bhavsar, a cosmic ray specialist and also a student of
Sarabhai's, had a PhD from PRL. He had studied high-
altitude cosmic rays using balloons at Minnesota. He
returned to India to join the space programme and was the
first Indian scientist to fly a sounding rocket payload from
Thumba. Thakore, an MSc in physics, had also studied
cosmic rays at PRL before going to Rochester to study
computers. He returned to India to become one of the
pioneers in computerization. Sarabhai roped him in to serve
ISRO. And he became Sarabhai's key man for budgeting and
financial planning.

Other pioneer scientists included Vasanth Gowariker,
a propellant engineer, who joined Thumba in 1967. He
had worked for the Atomic Energy Research Establishment
in the UK and the British Ministry of Aviation, and had
helped to build rocket motors for the British armed forces.
At ISRO, he was responsible for setting up the Propellant
Engineering Division and the Chemicals and Materials
Group. Suresh Chandra Gupta had studied in the Indian
Institute of Science, Bangalore, and had a doctorate in
electronics from the University of Pennsylvania. A specialist
in control and guidance systems and electronics, he had
spent several years in the US before landing in Trivandrum
in the mid-1960s.

Muthunayagam, the youngest in the group, was from nearby Nagarcoil, in Tamil Nadu. He was a brilliant mechanical engineer and a top ranker with an honours degree from the Madras University, a masters from the Indian Institute of Science and a doctorate from the University of Purdue. He was at NASA when Sarabhai met him and persuaded him to return to India. At ISRO later, Muthunayagam became the chief architect of rocket propulsion.

Y.J. Rao, an aeronautics engineer, had graduated from the Madras Institute of Technology and obtained a PhD in aeronautical engineering from the US. He had spent a number of years in the US before returning to India. He was the head of the aeronautics development activities in SSTC.

D.S. Rane was a gold medalist with a PhD in systems engineering. He was a professor in the US when Sarabhai picked him up for the space programme. At first Rane and his young family found it difficult to adjust to Trivandrum and he returned to his teaching job in the US. But the lure of working in this exciting new field drew him back. He rejoined ISRO and stayed on. He was initially in charge of systems engineering in SSTC. One of his major achievements was setting up the computational facilities at the Vikram Sarabhai Space Centre (VSSC), which was formed by integrating TERLS, SSTC, RFF and RPP after Sarabhai's death.

M.C. Mathur, a graduate of the Madras Institute of Technology, had also studied and worked in the US before joining ISRO in the late 1960s. He worked in aeronautics and quality assurance. V.P. Kulkarni, who had a PhD in electronics from Moscow University, joined Gupta in developing electronic systems for space.

Our small group of seven who had trained in NASA initially continued as part of the core team. H.G.S. Murthy, who was the first test director of TERLS, was the man on the spot for Sarabhai. We were joined by M.R. Kurup, a chemical engineer who had passed out of the DAE training school and worked in the chemistry division of DAE before he was deputed to space programme. Kurup was responsible for putting up the very first solid rocket propellant plant in the country at Trivandrum in the early 1960s.

U.R. Rao from Karnataka was also Sarabhai's student. He had worked at PRL and studied cosmic rays using American spacecraft during a stint at MIT. Sarabhai had earmarked him for setting up the satellite centre for space programme.

Our civil engineer R.D. John was deputed to space programme from the Madras PWD. He was our true pioneer as he was always the first man on the field in Thumba as well as Sriharikota, and was responsible for constructing the roads and buildings and other utilities.

In those early days our launches were simple affairs. Murthy would coordinate the overall launch activity. Easwaradas was in charge of the assembly and launch of the rockets. I headed the ground support division, which meant I was in charge of the ground instrumentation such as telemetry, radar tracking, timing and intercom. Kalam was the range safety officer, whose job was to make sure that land, sea and air were clear prior to the launch. His inputs for this were visual sightings, reports from the helicopter and sea vessel, and phone messages from the airport and other agencies.

The rocket and payload would be assembled and integrated in a small room. It would be transported to the launch pad by jeep while we cycled up to our assigned positions. Initially, the countdown was given from the bunker behind the pad and, later on, from the control room when we got one. We would stand at a safe distance away from the rocket and track it as it blasted off, streaked into the sky and finally fell into the Arabian Sea.

The initial launch campaigns provided plenty of learning opportunities especially when serious programmes were started to indigenize the hardware. We started in a small way to manufacture rockets, payloads, and instrumentation and ground systems. During this phase many incidents provided us with hard lessons.

I cannot forget the day when we were launching a small rocket which required a siren to be sounded three minutes before the launch. One of my colleagues pressed the siren switch a few minutes before the launch as a general warning! Suddenly a thundering noise was heard and the rocket had prematurely zoomed up. Murthy was heard asking anxiously what the big sound was about! After the initial shock, we started looking for casualties. Fortunately the rocket was pointing in the right direction when it took off and no one was hurt and no harm was done. We learned that day how important it was to isolate the ground leads of the firing circuits from the general electrical ground.

Then there was the series of Nike-Apache launches with vapour cloud payloads triggered by locally designed igniters. The rockets were to be fired successively. The first launch took off well, but there was no payload release. Determined not to be deterred by a single failure, the order was given to go ahead with the next firing. But, alas, that too was a failure. It then occurred to us to carefully examine the igniter in the laboratory. To our dismay, we found that while the igniter was fine under normal pressure, it did not work in a vacuum. The design was modified and in subsequent flights it functioned well.

There were, fortunately, no major accidents during those early launches, although there were cases when the rockets went astray and parts were picked up from the surrounding areas. We also worked out a regular system of compensation for fishermen who claimed their nets had been damaged by rocket debris.

By the mid-1960s, our sounding rocket launches were increasing in frequency and we were on a major expansion programme. Exciting new plans for the development of satellites and satellite launch vehicles were on the anvil. The team in charge of finding an east-facing site for launching big rockets had zeroed in on an island off the southern coast of Andhra. The new site, Sriharikota, was about 100 km north of Madras city. In the 1960s, Sriharikota was a remote, almost unapproachable island occupied only by the Yenadi tribals who lived in the forest. The Andhra government used this island for planting eucalyptus and casuarina trees which were then transported to places like Madras for use as firewood.

An east-facing site was sought so that we could get some additional impetus from the earth's rotational movement while launching satellites. The Andhra government provided large tracts of reserve forestland for the launch activity. They also actively helped in the acquisition of the required private land for the experimental launches as we would need a large safety zone to be cleared of human habitation in view of the hazardous nature of the proposed activities.

It was at this juncture that Sarabhai's first formal visit to Sriharikota was arranged in coordination with the Andhra government. Preliminary work for the visit, such as coordination with the state government, liaison with the local authorities, clearing of temporary jeep tracks in the forest area and so on, was undertaken by the civil engineers under the guidance of R.D. John, our site engineer. Since the legendary Buckingham Canal was to be traversed by the visiting team, the waterway traffic had to be suspended for a few days and a temporary bridge strong enough to allow the passage of jeeps had to be rigged up. This was done by stacking boats abreast and fixing sturdy wooden planks over them. This caused a pile-up of boats laden with cargo on either side of the temporary structure until the visit was over.

On the morning of the visit the retinue assembled at Sullurpeta where Sarabhai and other dignitaries were met by the Andhra government officials. Our team included senior personnel from Thumba, engineers and officials from DAE, Sarabhai and his close advisors including Chitnis, M.G.K. Menon, M.A. Vellodi and a host of other specialists. Somehow all our major ventures in those early years were destined to be baptized in churches, for it was in a church property that we first assembled even in Sullurpeta.

After a hearty breakfast, the team piled into a number of jeeps and moved in a convoy towards Pulicat Lake. It was summer and the water level was low. The vehicles could actually pass over the dry lake bed. The tough patches had been filled with dry leaves and branches by the advance team and the jeeps could pass through easily.

After a few kilometres we reached Buckingham Canal. The entire team had to get out of the vehicles so that the empty jeeps could cross the temporary bridge. We walked across and boarded the jeeps again to resume the trip. It was like a jungle safari. The freshly created track was made of logs hewn out of the forest trees, and the path was reinforced with branches and foliage cut and spread by the advance party.

It was quite an adventure for our young and energetic city crowd. The most enthusiastic was Sarabhai, who was in his late forties at that time. Many times the jeeps got stuck in the sand and we had to get out and push. A few vehicles broke down and had to be abandoned. One even caught fire and had to be doused with sand.

At long last the Bay of Bengal sparkled before us. We had covered just 20 km, but we felt as if we had battled through miles of jungle! We had got used to our little coastal station in Thumba with the gushing Arabian Sea and the lines of swaying coconut palms. But this beach was very different – and equally beautiful.

There wasn't too much time to savour the scenery, though. We got out of our jeeps and were given a quick briefing.

Then we started walking along the seashore, surveying possible locations for the launch pad and other associated structures. I was quite tired and so were my colleagues, but Sarabhai was as fresh as a breeze. Actually we found it difficult to keep pace with him as he covered almost 10 km by foot in the sand!

The coastal length of our new area was almost 40 km. The place had sporadic fishing activity. The local Yenadi who were native to the area were hunter-gatherers. For generations they had lived mainly on forest produce. Although they were a small group, they had to be protected and kept safe from the proposed launch activities.

The forest had a large acreage of casuarina plantations developed by the forest department and a wide variety of natural vegetation, mainly consisting of bushes and wild trees. A number of birds and animals including monkeys, jackals, rabbits and wild pigs roamed the forests. There were stories of occasional sightings of leopards and cheetahs. But what was remarkable was the presence of huge herds of wild cattle. Thousands of them roamed around freely all over the island. At that time we didn't know about the huge flocks of flamingoes and other exotic waterbirds, such as the painted storks and pelicans, which came to Pulicat in the winter.

We spent a few hours on the site and started back inland. After a gruelling drive we reached a forest rest house. A small gathering of tribals and local forest workers had been assembled by the local collector who had briefed them of the proposed visit of the VIPs.

The Yenadi were a totally isolated community. Many had not even seen a bicycle, as they had never gone out of the island. It was difficult to believe that this was the 1960s and we were standing on an island not too far from Madras. In retrospect I think the sight of so many vehicles and city folks must have been quite overwhelming for them. The Yenadi had been told that someone very important would address them. He would tell them about the great things the government would bring to the island and how it would benefit them. I think they assumed that Sarabhai was some kind of raja!

Sarabhai's English speech was translated for them by the district collector. He described his plans to them and told them that Sriharikota would become a nationally important place. They listened with great attention but I wonder if they really understood what he said! The Andhra government had arranged a ceremonial lunch in the local school building. It was like a grand wedding feast. Since Dr Sarabhai was a vegetarian the meal had the choicest of Andhra vegetarian delicacies.

Sarabhai asked the well-known architects Pithavadian and Partners to design the facilities and the associated housing colonies. Since Sriharikota was a cyclone prone area, the colony had to be built to withstand heavy winds and rain. Interestingly, the Yenadi who had lived there for generations had perfected their simple thatched structures by modifying their shapes to withstand the cyclones.

Soon R.D. John began work on the basic amenities on the island. The Sriharikota Range was ready by 1971. It was a modest facility by international standards; no one at that time would ever have imagined how rapidly it would grow, transforming into one of the most important spaceports in the world.

5

Early Learning Experiences from Around the World

While we were at NASA for training in sounding rocket assembly and launch at the Wallops station, Virginia, we used to pass through a restricted area where a major rocket launching pad was being operated. This was the largest pad at Wallops from where the all-solid launch vehicle, the Scout, was launched. These rockets were capable of orbiting a small 40 kg satellite into a low earth orbit.

That was in 1963 and we were all novices. We came to know much later that even at that time, when we had not even developed the capability of launching small sounding rockets, Sarabhai and Bhabha were already thinking of satellite launch capability. Around 1965 they had requested NASA for the know-how for building Scouts in India. Perhaps they were considering setting up a space launch facility in the country using the Scout as the first step. NASA agreed to sell a few Scouts to India purely for scientific research, but since the rockets had military potential, passing on the know-how was a strict no-no.

So, when Sarabhai asked the group of young engineers at SSTC to formulate plans to develop a modest satellite launch vehicle in the mid-1960s, the model was the Scout. Technologically, it was an extension of the sounding rocket development. Our R&D groups were already working on chemical formulations for efficient solid propellants. This was in addition to the French solid propellants for sounding rockets being manufactured under licence at RPP.

When Sarabhai took over DAE after the untimely death of Bhabha in 1966, the tempo of space research in India gained tremendous momentum. And since space was Sarabhai's first love, it began to receive considerable attention and funding. Sarabhai's famous 'Profile for the Decade 1970 to 1980' for the DAE and space research programme came out in 1970. This clearly spelled out the need for indigenous capability to make our own launch vehicles and satellites, and to launch them from our own soil by the mid-1970s. Sarabhai envisioned a synchronous satellite capability being in place by the end of the decade.

While the sounding rocket activity was on in full swing at TERLS, up Veli Hills, under Sarabhai's instructions, active preliminary design work was started around 1968 for identifying the Satellite Launch Vehicle (SLV) configuration. Various alternatives were suggested and a final choice was made of a configuration designated SLV-3, perhaps because it was the third alternative in the series of the suggested versions. This was an all-solid propellant four-stage rocket capable of orbiting a 30 to 40 kg satellite into 400 km circular orbit. It was around this time that the Indian Space Research Organization (ISRO) was formally notified under DAE.

Sarabhai asked Y.J. Rao, an experienced aeronautical engineer, to coordinate teams of specialists to carry out engineering designs of important elements of the vehicle and the launch facilities. These included all the four stages of the rocket, the heat shield, the avionics and guidance systems, the launch tower, the ground telemetry, radar tracking and telecommand, and the satellite itself.

The key engineers who led these design teams included Gowariker, Kurup, Muthunayagam, Kalam, Gupta, Madhavan Nair and U.R. Rao. I led the design team that worked on the tracking facilities. These young leaders went on to become legends in the saga of Indian space research. Kalam was eventually designated the project leader for the SLV-3 development.

Meanwhile in the early 1970s, Sarabhai decided to send Ramakrishna Rao, Y.J. Rao and me on a kind of world tour of several of the major space installations as well as component manufacturing units for an idea of the requirements for getting into the big league. It was an exciting time. We carefully planned our trip, with important inputs from Sarabhai and considerable research on our own.

Sarabhai had a unique way of functioning even in planning these visits. He just told the three of us to make a list of all the space stations and facilities around the world working on systems of relevance to us. When we gave him a detailed list of places to visit, he just signed on the dotted line without a single question. He was a man in a hurry and he knew the best way to motivate us was to show he trusted our judgement.

We had all travelled quite a bit before this, but our whirlwind world tour was something very unique. We took off from Trivandrum on a fine April day in 1970. Our first stop was DFVLR (now DLR), the German space agency in Munich which was mainly involved in coordinating between the German industries for the European space programmes. Ironically, DFVLR did not have any rocket development programmes of its own because of postwar restrictions. But we got to see their mobile facility which they used for launching sounding rockets. After our technical visit we had another learning experience. Our German colleagues took us to a monastery near a lake where monks served us beer and cheese. This, we learned, was the monastery where the famous German Oktober Fest originated.

Our next stop was Noordwijk in the Netherlands. We took a tram from The Hague and reached this town which housed some special labs in which the European Space Agency (ESA) built science payloads for satellites and rockets. Here we had a bad experience. When we landed there, to our shock and disappointment, the French chief of the establishment refused to even see us because he was 'too busy'. We stood there with our official letter dangling uselessly in our hands, not knowing what to do. Finally a British scientist took pity on us and took us on an abbreviated tour. It was not a very useful visit as there was little to see; plus, throughout, we were seething at the way we were treated.

Next came London close to where Rolls Royce had extensive facilities for rocket engine manufacturing. The high-precision mechanical fabrication facilities there were fascinating. We also felt quite at home with our hosts' crisp English and correct manners. It was such a welcome change and pleasure to visit an organization keen to do business with the Indian space agency.

By now we were quite starved for Indian food and so we decided to eat at the famous Veerasami's. They charged us a princely amount of 1.50 pounds for a vegetarian meal. We had our fill of vegetable biryani, curry and papad served in the proper British way. I also went to Bond Street and got myself a suit. Since we had some time on our hands, we decided to take a conducted tour of London and revisited all the traditional tourist spots –Trafalgar Square, Buckingham Palace, Piccadilly and the Tower Bridge.

From London we flew to Paris to visit the Centre national d'études spatiales (CNES). This was the headquarters of the French space programme as well as ESA. CNES had its office in the heart of Paris where we were briefed about their launch vehicle and satellite activity. With their extensive budgets and flourishing industries, they were the chief contributor to ESA. Later, we visited Toulouse in the south of France where CNES had a major R&D centre and some important aircraft manufacturing facilities.

Next on our schedule was the Centre Spatial Guyanais (CSG) or Guiana Space Centre in Kourou run by CNES. The twelve-hour non-stop flight from Paris to Cayenne, the capital of French Guiana, on board a Boeing 707 was quite tiring. From Cayenne to Kourou by road took another couple of hours. We were now about 15,000 miles away from India and the time difference was eleven hours.

We were put up in a luxury hotel, Des Roches, which charged us about 90 francs a day. This was much more than what we were being paid as per day allowance. But we had no choice, as there was no other place to stay. I also suddenly discovered that I was the sole interpreter for my colleagues, as French was the only language spoken over there.

I had never formally studied French, but a couple of years earlier, when Sarabhai deputed me to attend a month-long workshop in Paris I had assiduously studied all the phrase books and learned to communicate in French. Since I loved learning new languages, I kept in touch by reading the *Reader's Digest* in French! All this stood me in good stead at French Guiana.

This beautiful little spaceport belonging to France is located on the North Atlantic coast of South America. It borders Brazil to the east and south, and Suriname to the west. The centre had been operational for just two years when we went. The French had zeroed in on this particular location for their ambitious spaceport for two reasons. Since it was quite close to the equator the spinning earth could impart some extra velocity to the rockets when launched eastward. Also, since it had a large expanse of open sea to the east, the lower stages of rockets and debris from launch failures would not fall on human habitations.

In those days the Kourou facility was not as big as it is today. They were launching relatively small vehicles. The place was tropical and weather was similar to Trivandrum.

The space centre was the mainstay of the place. The economy was in poor shape as the sugar plantations had all been wiped out by disease. A fair number of the people there were of Indian origin, but they had settled there for generations and spoke only French and Tamil. They were very happy to see us and speak in Tamil and even invited us home for a meal. We were shown around the launch facility which was just being upgraded for larger rockets.

French Guiana had quite a long and dramatic history of occupation. The Amerindians, who were the indigenous people, were almost extinct. Now the amazingly well-integrated population was made up of several races that had lived there for centuries: Africans who had come as slaves, Indians who had been employed as indentured labour in the plantations, Dutch whose ancestors had occupied the territory once, French whose forefathers had either owned the plantations or were escaped prisoners from the 'penitentiary' on Devil's Island close by. Added to this mix were the Brazilians who had trickled in across the border.

French Guiana was an idyllic place with a fantastic variety of butterflies and birds. Devil's Island, the notorious penitentiary, had closed long ago and been turned into a tourist attraction. It had housed several interesting prisoners. The most famous of these was Henri Charrière whose book *Papillon* had just been released in 1969. In this memoir, which became an instant bestseller, he described his escape from the island. Unfortunately we had no time to explore the surrounding areas.

We did not watch any launches, but we got a good idea of what we should look out for while setting up a major launch station. By now we were beginning to understand why Sarabhai had sent us on this tour. We were learning first-hand about the huge potential of space technology which went much beyond our small sounding rockets.

We had one small adventure before we reached our next stop, New York. We got stuck overnight at the Port of Spain, Trinidad, while transiting through to New York. Some political turmoil had resulted in a dusk-to-dawn curfew and so our flight could not take off. We were put up in a good hotel and were told we could reach the airport safely in the morning. I decided to enjoy my providential Caribbean holiday! After the lightning trips in Europe, my stay at Kourou seemed like a convalescence holiday. I could now see why the French wanted to launch their satellites from Kourou although it was halfway across the globe for them.

We stopped over at New York on the way to Washington, DC. From DC we went to the Langley Research Centre of NASA and then on to good old Wallops station. This NASA centre in Virginia where I worked for about a year in 1963 had not changed much. We met some old friends after seven years.

We returned to spend a day at the Goddard Space Flight Centre in DC, before leaving for Cape Kennedy and then moving on to Houston. In a letter to my fiancée Gita, I wrote:

It has been a mad rush these last few weeks. Am in fine health, although a bit tired. It is nice to have been able to visit so many installations in different countries and to be in a position to compare and evaluate various facilities. Such an opportunity is quite rare especially to a foreigner I guess! There seems to be a lot of rumpus here in the Universities because of Nixon's Cambodia policies. As a matter of fact I was watching from the window of a friend's house the goings on in the University of Maryland's campus, near Washington DC. The police were throwing smoke bombs from helicopters on the students (more girls than boys), and there was a lot of shooting going on!

Our next stop was the Kennedy Space Centre. Originally known as Cape Canaveral, this space station is situated in Florida on the East Coast of the US. It was briefly renamed Cape Kennedy from 1963 to 1973 (which was when we visited) and later on reverted to its original name.

Those were the days when the moon landing and Apollo programmes were at their peak. We were stunned by the scale and size of the structures at the manned mission launch facility at Kennedy. What impressed us most was how a small number of people were operating such huge hardware. We were taken up in the elevators that carried the astronauts to their capsules and shown how the world looks down below. We were also awed by the sight of huge boosters being handled by cranes and pulleys, and the efficiency with which the stages of the large rockets were assembled. India was still in the sounding rocket phase then and I never dreamed that one day, in the not-too-far-off future, I would be the director of a homegrown satellite launch facility in India where we would be doing all this and more!

Our next stop was the Houston Manned Space Center (now the Lyndon B. Johnson Space Center) in Texas. This was the nerve centre for communication with astronauts during manned missions. Experts sitting here controlled the activities of astronauts, instructed them on what to do and handled on-board emergencies. It was an incredible experience seeing them in continuous voice contact with space stations around the world and in communication with astronauts in orbit.

At Huntsville, Alabama, our next stop, we got to see NASA's facilities for large liquid and cryogenic propulsion engine development. The Marshall Space Flight Center was the leading centre for liquid propulsion engine development for large rockets. It all looked almost like science fiction to us then. We never imagined we would ever have anything like that in India.

Incidentally this was where Wernher Von Braun did his Saturn rocket development. So, apart from the technical facilities, we also got to see an exclusive museum devoted to Von Braun, showcasing his life right from his brilliant student days to his work on the famous V2 rockets for Hitler and his work on Saturn rockets for NASA.

The Western Test Range in California is an important launch facility of NASA. Our visit here gave us some special insights as it was a typical launch base with all the range instrumentation we would need to build at Sriharikota

– which at that moment was just an unoccupied island earmarked for a future launch station.

We moved on next to the Jet Propulsion Laboratory, a NASA-funded facility for space technology R&D located in Pasadena near San Francisco. This centre, which had a typical university atmosphere, was home to an elite academic community. The focus here was on state-of-the-art work in a wide range of rocket- and satellite-related fields. We found the academics slightly secretive since the work they were doing was classified. But we did learn a lot about the importance of teamwork in a high-tech R&D organization.

From San Francisco we returned to Los Angeles and contacted the NASA representative. Ramakrishna Rao and I, the two tracking specialists, were picked up from our hotel and driven to the airport where a small six-seater plane awaited us. I had never flown in such a tiny aircraft before! The bumpy ride was really scary. At NASA's famous Goldstone Tracking Station in the Mojave Desert, we were shown the giant antennas used for tracking moon rockets and other planetary objects, and got the chance to examine the cutting-edge electronic and communication equipment. We flew back to LA in quite a dazed condition!

From San Francisco we flew to Honolulu to visit the downrange tracking station in Hawaii. We were welcomed at the airport in typical Hawaiian style with the traditional garland called the lei and a drink of pineapple juice. After checking into our hotel, we found ourselves with some free time before our meeting, so we decided to visit the Waikiki beach. Since there was no time to change, we took a stroll down the famous beach fully and formally dressed in our suits. We must have seemed a strange trio as we walked self-consciously along the sandy strip teeming with semi-naked bathers and strollers.

The next morning we flew to another Hawaiian island called Kuwaii where the tracking systems were located. We were shown around the small but well-organized facility used for the downrange tracking of rockets and satellites launched by NASA. The Kaena Point Satellite Tracking Station on the island of Oahu in Hawaii is another remote tracking station of the Air Force Satellite Control Network responsible for tracking satellites in orbit. The station originally opened in 1959 to support Corona, an early reconnaissance satellite programme. It was a beautiful facility placed near the westernmost point of the island, atop a 1500-foot high ridge. The two radomes, locally known as the 'golf balls', were a popular landmark for fishing vessels in the surrounding waters.

Japan was our last and final stop. We went first to the University of Tokyo which was the coordinating agency for the Japanese rocket development programme in those days. The professor in charge of the programme gave us a briefing. But when we asked to meet Professor Itokawa, the man who had been so closely associated with the Indian space programme, we were told he had moved. We tried to contact him directly, but for some mysterious reasons he was reluctant to meet us. Later, we learned that he was under investigation. I never knew what exactly happened to him. We had some time to go sightseeing around Tokyo and had a ride in the bullet train, introduced just a couple of years earlier.

From Tokyo, we flew to the city of Osaka and drove to the Uchinoura Space Centre in the Kagoshima Prefecture. It was a rather remote area fronting the Pacific Ocean in the south of Japan. Imagine our shock and surprise when we reached to find the place totally deserted! It was quite eerie – not a single other person was in sight. And yet we knew several launches had taken place from there quite recently. After some hunting around we found a sleepy middle-aged man who looked very puzzled to see us.

With a lot of sign language and trial and error, we managed to communicate with him. We learned that during non-launch days the range was shut down. It was commissioned only during launch campaigns when teams of scientists from Tokyo descended a few weeks ahead and operated the facility. Our guide opened each facility laboriously and explained the set-up as best he could. Japan's space activities in those days were fairly modest and somewhat in the same scale as what we were planning and so the visit was quite instructive. We came away amazed at how they managed to keep such a facility operational with just one man holding the fort for most of the time!

The originally planned Australian leg of our trip got cancelled. But I went to Australia soon after under very different circumstances.

After a series of failures of its developmental launches from the Woomera range in Australia, the European Launcher Development Organisation (ELDO) had decided to abandon its plan to develop an all-European satellite launch vehicle. This was in the late 1960s. The ambitious programme which held out so much promise had to be scrapped because the various participating countries had their own personal agendas and could not make this cooperative venture work.

In 1970, Dr Sarabhai received information that the organization was scrapping brand-new satellite telemetry and tracking stations, and putting them up for auction. He thought this was a great opportunity for us to acquire the systems at a low price for our own programmes in India.

One day Murthy received a call from Sarabhai asking him to depute my colleague Ramakrishna Rao and I to visit the remote northern Australian station called Gove where the auction was being held. We were to inspect the system and bid for it. In order to bid at the auction, we had to collect foreign exchange from the Reserve Bank of India (RBI) in Bombay and then proceed to Australia where Murthy would join us.

Everything happened very fast. We reached Bombay and were asked to go to the RBI directly. We called on the RBI official and explained our requirement. Those were the days of stringent forex regulations and severe scarcity of hard currency. The RBI official looked at us in disbelief. The audacity of these two unknowns who were demanding the release of forex and that too in the form of an open demand draft for bidding at a foreign auction! It was unheard-of and he brusquely told us to leave.

We did not know what to do. Since the auction was imminent, we decided to telephone Sarabhai directly and give him the bad news – it never occurred to us that he might be too busy to take our call. Sarabhai came on the line and told us to stay put and wait in the outer office of the bank – he would get back to us, he said.

Sure enough, we had a response very soon. Not from Sarabhai, but from the same official who had asked us to get out. He rushed out from his office and asked us to accompany him inside. He requested us very politely to wait for a few minutes and said the demand draft would be ready. He wanted to know in whose name the draft should be made.

We followed him dumbfounded, wondering at his sudden transformation. It was only much later that we learned that Sarabhai had telephoned the Union finance minister Y.B. Chavan, who in turn had personally telephoned the poor official and got the forex released so fast – all this had happened while we were standing in the corridor!

Ramakrishna Rao and I landed in Darwin as scheduled. We were joined by Murthy, and the three of us flew to Gove.

And then we got our second shock!

Gove looked like some kind of abandoned army barracks. A group of brawny men eyed us curiously as we got out of our hired vehicle. We had no clue who they were. Had they come for the auction? Were they security guards? They certainly didn't look like engineers.

'Who are you? Where have you come from? Why are you here?' one of them asked after a while.

We explained that we had heard the space station had been closed and we were space scientists who had come all the way from India to bid in the auction for the equipment.

'All the way from India!' he repeated incredulously. 'Didn't you know the auction is over?'

What! We were absolutely shocked and disappointed.

Looking around us, we could not see any equipment. 'At least we should try and see what we have missed after coming all this way,' Murthy murmured to us. He asked the man to show us where the equipment was.

Then came our next shock. We were shown a whole array of racks and antenna structures dismantled and piled up in the yard. Our impromptu guide told us they had decided no one would be interested in buying the highly specialized equipment second-hand. So it had all been broken up into bits and sold to scrap dealers!

We were devastated that all our efforts had gone to waste. There was no official-looking person in sight. We didn't know what to do next. We had travelled a long way and I needed to use the toilet. I asked our 'guide' to show me where I should go and he pointed towards a building. I opened the door and got my next big shock. It was a big communal toilet and all the men inside were walking around stark naked, laughing, talking, arguing, and also using the loo!

I quickly used the loo and ran out. I had never seen such a sight before!

We finally located the person in charge and told him about our journey. And then we got our next surprise – a pleasant one this time. He said this tracking station had been sold for scrap as there were no takers for the equipment. But the good news was that there was one more tracking station in southern Australia that was still intact and we could have a look at that. If we were interested we could negotiate the price and buy it off them. There would be no auction and no other bidders. And he said they would even fly us over at their own cost to south Australia.

The next day, rested and fed, we set off on the next leg of our adventure. It was a memorable trip, spanning the whole beautiful continent. From Adelaide in the south where we landed, we went across to another remote tracking station. Here we finally managed to negotiate the purchase of a complete ground station at about 10 per cent of its original cost and arranged to ship it to Madras. It was an excellent deal, and to top it all, the DD from the Reserve Bank which we had obtained with so much difficulty was not even needed as we had to pay for the equipment only later, after it was shipped to India.

And so it was that we got our first telemetry ground station for Sriharikota. My colleague Ved Prakash Sandlas went to Australia and familiarized himself with the equipment. He also supervised its packing and shipment and finally got it installed in SHAR. What we got was a very basic telemetry station, but it was more than sufficient for our programme at that time.

In 1970 we also had our first significant collaboration with the Russians. The M-100 programme was a collaborative project with the Hydrometeorological Services, which is the equivalent of the India Meteorological Department. Russia had extensive facilities for meteorological forecasts. Apart from their ground-based services, they also had a network of meteorological rocket launchers on land and on ships, scattered across locations all over the world.

India had agreed to launch M-100 rockets from Thumba every week in synchronization with other Russian sites so that a simultaneous set of data could be obtained. It was also agreed that data from all the sites would be freely disseminated to all scientists from anywhere in the world who wanted it. This was essentially a scientific mission and there was no element of technology transfer.

Although the Thumba scientists could carry out the entire operation by themselves, the Russian personnel were always in the rocket range supervising the launches. For a long time they would not let us Indians handle their equipment. But we didn't really mind. Since we were all part of the launch team, there was considerable camaraderie amongst us. And so it was that, at any point of time for years to come, there were always a few Russians hanging around enjoying the sea and the balmy weather. They made friends with the local people and were generally well liked by the Thumba staff.

More than a thousand M-100 rockets were launched between 1970 and 1993. These rockets were used to collect regular temperature and wind speed data up to an altitude of about 80 km. They were systematically launched every single week on a regular basis. The data was collected and passed on to an international data centre where it was used for generating a worldwide meteorology picture. We might not have made any dramatic discoveries but we learned a lot from this exercise. We collected a huge bank of useful data over nearly a quarter of a century. This helped us to understand weather patterns in this area.

The M-100 launches had another interesting spin-off. Since they were launched every single Wednesday without fail at exactly the twilight hour, we would have hundreds of spectators coming over to Thumba to watch the take-off. What started off as a trickle of interested people, and maybe some fishermen, grew over the years. Schools and colleges sent their students; employees brought their families; people from all over Trivandrum applied for passes to bring their visitors from outside to watch the take-off. They never tired of coming again and again to watch the launch vehicle zoom off across the beautiful Arabian Sea, sometimes under a starlit sky and sometimes sheathed in heavy rain.

In 1969, the Americans landed on the moon, at a time when we were still launching our sounding rockets. Like everyone else in India we too followed the news of the moon landing avidly. Little did we know that one day we ourselves would launch spacecraft to the moon, and to Mars and beyond!

The American astronauts had returned to earth with some rocks picked up from the surface of the moon. Everyone was excited. What would the moon rock look like? Would we ever get to see it? Could we touch it? The Americans decided to be generous – pieces of moon rock were dispatched all over the world and exhibited at select locations in tightly sealed glass cases. These exhibitions drew huge crowds.

And then we heard that a piece of moon rock was coming to Thumba. It was to be a big event, but only for the employees since we thought no one else would be interested. Sarabhai was coming with other senior colleagues from Ahmedabad. Kenneth Keating, the US ambassador to India, was flying down to inaugurate the event.

The rock arrived in its glass case. It was the size of a walnut. We set it up in the foyer of SSTC on top of Veli Hills. The programme was finalized: Keating would give a speech, followed by Sarabhai and some of the others, and then all the employees could file past and take a look at the rock. But we had reckoned without the frenzy of public interest that had been stirred up when the local newspapers announced the arrival of the moon rock in Trivandrum.

I was on top of Veli Hills as part of the committee arranging the display of the rock when a colleague called out to me.

'Dan,' he said, 'just take a look at this!'

I went to where he was standing. A huge crowd of people was surging up the hill towards us. They came in vehicles, on foot, by bicycle, by bus. Obviously no one in Trivandrum wanted to miss this opportunity to catch a glimpse of the extraterrestrial material!

'This is a once-in-a-lifetime opportunity, saar,' one of the employees said. He was standing next to me watching the crowd coming up the hill. 'When will they ever get such a chance again? Even my family has come. They are somewhere there in the crowd.'

We were quite unprepared. As the crowds grew it became a law and order problem and we had to call for help from the police and civil authorities.

But it all ended well. Ambassador Keating inaugurated the exhibition and gave a good speech. The crowds were allowed in soon after for a glimpse of the rock. There were glowing reports in the papers the next morning. The moon rock had found its own special place in the hearts of the people of Trivandrum.

6

The Growing Years

Kalam and I had become close friends as we were the only bachelors from the original group. We both continued to live in the same lodge: the 'famous' Indra Bhavan, near the Trivandrum Secretariat. This lodge housed bachelors from all over the country who had come to work in this new, exciting field.

Since both of us were vegetarians, we would most often end up having dinner together in any of the small eateries dotting the one and only 'Main Road' of Trivandrum. Although Kalam was a vegetarian, he loved the egg masala with parotta at Xavier's Hotel on the Main Road near the Secretariat. Otherwise we would eat in any of the bhavans which served idli and dosa. Our favourite eating place, ironically, was the railway station canteen which served Tamil Nadu style meals with cooked rice, as against the parboiled rice which the Malayalis preferred.

When we arrived in Trivandrum in the early 1960s, 'outsiders' like us were a rarity. In fact, any man wearing a shirt and trousers would be deemed a Thumba employee!

The sudden influx of so many young people from all over the country was a bit of a culture shock to the locals. We bachelors had nothing much to do during the weekends. During launch campaigns, of course, there were no weekends or holidays. But at other times, we would either go to the beaches at Kovalam or Shankumukham or catch an old Hollywood movie at the Srikumar Theatre. Kalam, who came from Rameswaram, loved to swim and he would spend hours on the beach at Kovalam.

In the late 1960s, our office rented a beautiful old colonial building called Ingledine, opposite the Trivandrum Raj Bhavan and converted it into the Rocket Recreation Club (RRC) with two badminton courts, a table tennis table and a room for card players. Kalam, like the rest of us, was an enthusiastic badminton player. We all got involved in setting up the club, buying furniture and getting a canteen going. Every evening we had friendly badminton matches, with the losers having to stand the winners a bonji (which is how a glass of lime juice was referred to in Trivandrum). We had decided not to serve liquor. Chellappan, the cook we hired, was famous for his exotic dishes such as tender coconut pudding.

For the young families coming from different parts of the country it was difficult to adjust to the slow-paced life in a town which seemed to belong to a different era and where people spoke only in Malayalam. But soon all of us adjusted to Trivandrum and we became full-fledged Trivandrumites. Trivandrum had many attractions. It was a small and compact city with solid educational institutions and medical facilities. In fact, many of my colleagues like Gupta, Rane and Kulkarni who came from very different parts of India settled down in Trivandrum after they retired.

In 1970 I got married to Gita, a young journalist. Kalam and Easwaradas were the first of my friends she met as soon as she landed. Since Easwaradas was a family man, he and his wife helped us set up our home. Kalam and my other bachelor friends hosted a dinner for her at Mascot Hotel.

On his first visit to Trivandrum after we got married, Dr Sarabhai threw a party for some visiting dignitaries and I introduced my wife to him. In typical Sarabhai style he asked her all about herself and what she wrote, and asked her to show him all her press clippings. 'Maybe you can also become part of our programme in some way,' he said, and Gita came away glowing and feeling very special!

She was so inspired that she decided to write an article on Thumba for the now defunct but iconic *The Illustrated Weekly of India*. Khushwant Singh, who was the editor then, agreed immediately. The only problem was that she needed a typewriter. Until then she had always used office typewriters in the newspaper offices she worked in. My friend Kalam came to the rescue. He had bought a portable while he was in the US and wasn't using it, so he offered to lend it to Gita for as long as she wanted.

Since it was the capital of a politically volatile state, Trivandrum offered Gita excellent writing opportunities. But the city was also a strange amalgam. On the one hand, it was a conservative society where women did not drive cars or even ride bicycles or scooters. Gita driving around the narrow roads of Trivandrum was a source of great amazement and amusement to the locals who would exclaim, '*Ayyo, sthree car otikinnu!*' (Ayyo, a woman is driving a car!) On the other hand, the women were highly educated compared to other parts of the country and often had good jobs. For example, whenever we went to the Trivandrum Engineering College for recruitment we would always be able to pick up a couple of bright young women engineers for ISRO.

There was one unforgettable episode for Gita when Kalam came to her 'rescue' at the first ever launch she witnessed in Thumba. We had scheduled to launch at dawn a Nike-Apache Sounding Rocket. Easwaradas had offered to drive us over in his car as Gita was also coming. We had to be there a little past midnight so we could be ready to launch at dawn. By now we had a good launch pad and bunkers and most importantly a control centre.

The control centre, in which I also had an office, was a round building abutting the sea. It had a nice terrace from which visitors could witness the launch. We dropped Gita off at the control centre. Two of our other colleagues, Sandlas and Bahl, had also brought their newly-wed wives. Leaving her in good company, I went off to the launch pad.

Rajarathnam, a young engineer from Karnataka, was our permanent countdown man as he had a stylish way of making the announcements. We had small speakers fixed on the terrace so visitors could follow our countdown. There were some people watching from the beach as well. I was in my tracking station.

The launch was going on schedule. All stations had given a 'Roger' and Rajarathnam began his countdown. 10-9-8-7-6-5-4-3-2-1 and… the rocket *didn't* take off!

I rushed from my tracking station to the launch pad in a jeep and became immersed in trying to figure out what had gone wrong. Meanwhile, Gita soon found herself all alone on the terrace of the control centre. The other husbands had collected their wives. She came down to find that the centre was deserted. Rajarathnam had gone home and the security person was waiting for her to go out so he could lock the door.

She went out to the beautiful beach and stood by the small driveway, unable to savour even the beauty of the breaking dawn and the swells of the waves. All she could think of was that she was in a totally deserted place and didn't know where to go. Just then a jeep drove up and Kalam hopped out.

'What are you doing here all alone?' he asked. When he heard her story he burst out laughing. 'Trust my buddy to forget he got married,' he said. 'He must have buried his head in the rocket. Come, let us go find him!'

Sure enough they found me with my hand inside the rocket trying to fix the switch which had misbehaved. Kalam packed me into the jeep with Gita. The story ended well, after all – she came back the next day and the rocket did take off!

Trivandrum in the 1970s had many beautiful and spacious houses with small gardens and the rents were particularly low when compared to other cities. The Gulf boom was just starting. People working abroad were building modern houses in their hometowns where they planned to come and settle one day. We found one such house in Vazhuthacaud.

Kalam would often come to our house to eat. He loved traditional Iyengar food like *vendhya kozhambu* and *puliyogare*. He also loved to talk to Gita about his favourite book, *Atlas Shrugged*, and its hero, who was his ideal. He would also talk about his dream of building a hovercraft in his backyard. He always intended to take a house with a big yard and get to work on it. Somehow that never happened. The SLV project got going and it took all his time – and, before he knew it, he was in a different orbit.

One of our favourite projects was to find a suitable girl for Kalam. We would often discuss this and even plan how we would hire a huge bus and all drive over to Rameswaram for his wedding. But somehow this was one project that never materialized.

A concerted recruitment drive had begun at a furious pace during the late 1960s and early '70s. The activities focused around Trivandrum and soon spread to other centres like Bangalore, Sriharikota and Ahmedabad. The numbers increased from a mere handful in the early 1960s to more than 16,000 in subsequent decades.

Indra Bhavan brimmed with young engineers, bachelors in their early twenties, who had come from all over the country. Others had young families and settled in lovely houses with tree-filled gardens. Since, initially, we didn't have a colony, the families were scattered all over the town and they soon blended with the local community. A rather interesting spin-off was the mushrooming of several cultural organizations these people created. By the mid-1970s we had Bengali, Marathi, Telugu, Kannada, Tamil and Hindi associations. Krishnamurthy, a young local engineer working in Thumba, started Soorya, a cultural association which became a phenomenal success within a short span of time.

Soorya brought music and dance programmes, films and plays from all over the country. Krishnamurthy also managed to get artistes, film-makers and choreographers to come and address the audiences which mainly comprised of people from Thumba. All these associations certainly enriched the cultural life of the city.

But, side by side, we were all getting more and more involved in our specialized spheres of work. The sounding rocket launches were becoming more infrequent; the influx of foreign scientists had dwindled into a trickle. The focus was shifting to bigger rockets and spacecraft.

At TERLS, we the pioneers were wearing many hats each by now. As the chief of the ground support division, I was in charge of tracking and telemetry. But I was head of several other sections as well: test and evaluation, communications, photography, library, security, stores and purchase... just two heads short of Ravana, I would joke! I had a cycle and before each launch I would cycle from the control centre to the radar and telemetry stations to make sure everything was fine.

As a bunch of enthusiastic youngsters we were anxious to fly our systems as soon as the laboratory models worked and the flight models were packaged. This was fine in the very early years when we used very simple sounding rockets, but we realized very soon that it was vital to have an independent authority to test and evaluate the subsystems that go into a rocket before incorporating it into a bigger mission. This realization came to us rather early in the programme, in a somewhat dramatic fashion.

In the 1960s, fresh from our spell of training at NASA we were keen to quickly indigenize at least some parts of the rocket payloads. The first one we tried was an electronic timer that would trigger various events in the course of the rocket's flight. We developed a timer with the available components, and after cursory laboratory testing – during which the package had worked perfectly – declared it to be suitable for flying. What we did not account for was the effect of the launch pad heating during the countdown. The timer was set to go off at about seventy seconds. During the flight we observed that the actual firing time of the timer was above 100 seconds – much longer than we had anticipated. We learned that day that the system had to be tested on the ground over a range of temperatures. We had to redesign the circuitry so that it would remain stable in this range. And the penalty we paid was the precious loss of data for those thirty-odd seconds.

Another instance in the early days was that of the sodium vapour payload developed by Kalam and his team. In this, sodium pellets were packed in a canister in the sounding rocket and fired by an igniter during the course of the flight. This resulted in the release of the sodium in the form of a vertical trail which was then photographed from three or more locations for computing the upper atmospheric winds. The handling and filling of sodium in itself was a highly hazardous process and we had had some serious (but not fatal) accidents during our laboratory trials. Anyway, we had successfully developed the canister and conducted many ground firings.

Then came the launch campaign when we had to fly a series of sodium payloads alternately at dawn and dusk. The rockets employed for the campaign were Nike-Apache sounding rockets made by NASA. The first rocket in the series was launched, but alas, the sodium did not eject. A quick post-launch review attended by Kalam, Murthy, me and some others concluded that this was a random failure. We decided to proceed with another launch the next day.

Lo and behold, that was also a failure. So, obviously the failure was not random. Kalam decided to go back to the drawing board and see what was wrong. We tested the igniter in the laboratory and it worked fine. Then someone had a brainwave. Could the vacuum environment have something to do with the problem? The igniter was then mounted inside a bell jar and fired. To our surprise it failed! We then realized we had lost two expensive rockets because of a simple problem. It took very little effort to rectify the defect and proceed with the programme. The lessons we learned as engineers and as an organization from these episodes were quite vital to our future programmes.

There was concern at the highest levels at the organic changes needed to avoid these mistakes. Thus, in the 1960s, was born the very first test and evaluation (T&E) division in ISRO, and the task of steering it was assigned to me since I was relatively independent of the payload development teams and could be thus quite objective in certifying the products. I had a small team to assist me full-time in this. My first deputy was K.V. Venkatachary who was with me in TERLS looking after our small T&E lab. Later, he moved to

Sriharikota and became a pioneer of the ISRO tracking and telemetry network.

The launch of the first sounding rocket from Thumba on 21 November 1963 marked the official beginning of the Indian space programme. But it was the formal dedication of TERLS to the UN on 2 February 1968 that gave the real impetus to developmental activities. Although we had been working for some time on developing indigenous technology, it was on that day that Sarabhai clearly outlined his plans for our nascent space group. The dedication ceremony was a grand one. We had spent weeks preparing for it. Scientists had come from all over the world. Prime Minister Indira Gandhi who was the chief guest did the formal dedication. Secretary General U Thant could not make it. And Sarabhai's chief guide and mentor Homi Bhabha was no more.

I spent most of the time in my trailer, in order to demonstrate our tracking abilities to the visiting dignitaries. But for all of us, there was a palpable sense of excitement – a feeling that we were on the threshold of something magnificent.

Sarabhai's iconic speech said it all. I reproduce here two small excerpts which illustrate what a visionary he was.

> The illustrated brochure, which is distributed here, reflects activities at the range. Advanced technology developing side by side with the little child close to nature; radars capable of tracking small fast moving objects at great distances and a nose cone being transported on a bicycle – these truly form the pattern

of modern India. There are some who question the relevance of space activity in a developing nation. To us, there is no ambiguity of purpose. We do not have the fantasy of competing with economically advanced nations in the explorations of the moon and the planets or manned space flight. But we are convinced that if we are to play a meaningful role nationally, and in the comity of nations, we must be second to none in the application of advanced technologies to the real problems of man and society, which we find in our own country.

And he made another very important point.

One of the most important benefits of space research lies in the spin-off which follows. I might illustrate this from the experience which we are gaining in the development of rockets. This involves new disciplines and an understanding of materials and methods; of close tolerances and testing under extremes; the development of guidance and control and the use of advanced information techniques. When one succeeds, it is through the working together of a large number of specialists who dedicate themselves to a common task. Indeed, I often feel that the discipline and the culture of the new world which emerges through the pursuit of activities of this type are among the most important from the standpoint of a developing nation.

Sarabhai was in a hurry to get things going. So, even as we were launching the foreign-made Nike-Apaches and Centaures, he simultaneously wanted us to start building our own rocket motors. By 1964 Sarabhai had signed an agreement with Sud Aviation, a French firm, to manufacture Centaure sounding rockets under licence and to ultimately supply them to France. Obviously he had great trust in our capabilities because this was done at a time when we barely even knew what went into making a rocket!

So, even while experiments continued with foreign-made rockets, parallel plans to manufacture Indian-made Centaures were initiated. DAE was roped in to set up a Rocket Fabrication Facility (RFF) for the manufacture of mechanical hardware and a Rocket Propellant Plant (RPP) for making the solid propellant blocks. The goal was to eventually integrate the ready-to-fly rockets right there in Trivandrum.

But that was not all. Sarabhai was already dreaming of entering the satellite-launching field. At the SSTC, groups of young men started working on the R&D of a multitude of subsystems for our Satellite Launch Vehicle (SLV) programme. Multi-disciplinary groups were set up with expertise which could also feed into the development of indigenous sounding rockets. Visiting scientists were extremely impressed by the variety of scientific knowledge available in a single location.

Plans were afoot to develop and manufacture a spectrum of sounding rockets in India to cover various altitudes and payloads. This project was christened the Rohini Sounding

Rocket (RSR) programme. The idea was to make these standard rockets and keep them in store to be provided to the scientists as and when they needed them. In addition the project would also fabricate standard payload elements as building blocks. The SSTC groups were quite active at this time: a large number of configurations were suggested and some of them were actually tried out with varying degrees of success.

On the face of it, developing a small sounding rocket might seem quite simple compared to large boosters and satellite launch vehicles. But our initial experience was the opposite: our small rockets created big problems for us!

The meteorological rockets were quite tiny compared to their big brothers. They had a diameter of about just 200 mm. However, their very smallness made them fly with very high acceleration and this created all sorts of problems. A major concern was the propellant. It had to burn properly without getting extinguished or becoming unstable. The structure also had to withstand the sudden high aerodynamic forces without breaking up. Most importantly the payload had to survive the vibration and accelerations and perform as required.

We were an inexperienced bunch of youngsters and we found the task extremely challenging. After a great deal of experimentation, the RSR project finally zeroed in on three versions of Rohini sounding rockets. The RH 200, which went up to an altitude of 80 km, was to be used to cover meteorology. The RH 300, which could fly up to 160 km altitude, was meant for aeronomy studies in the lower altitudes and the RH 560, which could go up to 470 km, was to be used for aeronomy in the higher altitudes.

The payload capability covered a range varying from 8 to 100 kg depending on the rocket. The experience gained in developing these rockets had another important spin-off. The teams actively engaged in the SLV design and development had a ready platform to try out some of their systems as well as the hardware and software.

Thus propellants could be tried out as well as the propulsion systems, igniters, payload deployment mechanisms, separation systems and onboard avionics subsystems. For example, we used an RH 560 rocket to test out a control system package or a combination of RH 200 and RH 300 rockets to validate the design of strap-on techniques. These concepts were successfully proved and later applied to larger motors.

There were, of course, some dramatic failures during the course of these developments – some benign and some leading to major accidents. I have already mentioned the case of a small rocket taking off prematurely when a safety siren was sounded a few minutes prior to the intended take-off. There were also a few cases when rockets went off course, sometimes into inhabited areas. Fortunately no one was hurt in any of these incidents. I also remember the case of a rocket nose cone ejecting right on the launch pad during the countdown owing to some false triggering.

And then there were the accidents which occurred during the manufacture of rocket hardware and devices. The most tragic was a fatal accident in the RFF during the proof pressure testing of a rocket casing on the shop floor. Due to our inexperience, we set up a pneumatic pressure test rig instead of the safer hydraulic set-up. The casing was subjected to very high pressures due to erroneous gauging. This resulted in the parts of the case dislodging and the debris hitting an operator who died instantly. Two others were struck by the pressure wave and lost their eyesight.

There was also a serious accident during the preparation of sodium pellets resulting in severe burns and injury to senior engineers. Fortunately it did not result in fatalities. There were many non-lethal failures, some because of faulty material and others due to faulty design.

Similarly, as we have seen, it took a couple of failed flights and much brainstorming before we identified the lack of vacuum testing as the problem behind the series of sounding rocket payload failures carrying the indigenously made sodium payloads. And we learned the hard way from other failed flights that certain relays used in the payload were highly sensitive to shock forces during the take-off. They would switch off the payloads a few milliseconds after take-off, resulting in a failed flight.

The lessons learned from these failures were enormous. We not only had to correct and improve the hardware but also reorganize our overviewing and certifying set-up. A very important outcome was the emergence of a quality and reliability group totally independent of the design and operational ones. I started this activity with the available experienced personnel to carry out test and evaluation as well as quality audit. This core group of a handful of engineers grew to a large group of more than 300 persons and, later, served as a model for all other centres of ISRO in the establishment of similar groups.

Coming back to sounding rockets, over the decades, the tempo of launches slowed down. The number of scientists wishing to carry out exclusive rocket soundings was dwindling. The progress made in other modes of observation, such as satellite-based experiments or technologically advanced ground observations, caught the attention of these scientists who had to use their budgets carefully.

All this certainly had its impact on ISRO as well. In a way this was helpful since the manpower and facilities were now diverted more effectively for SLV and spacecraft development. In fact, many of the pioneers of the sounding rocket programme moved on to lead other important projects of ISRO.

7

Sarabhai

I had met Dr Sarabhai quite a few times after my first encounter with him in Ahmedabad. But I got to know him at a more personal level only after I came to Trivandrum.

He was a handsome man. But, more importantly, he was a brilliant and charismatic person with a fantastic memory. This combination attracted his young engineers as they felt he was always so approachable – a man who never bothered about the usual social formalities.

He had his trademark dress. Although he was dressed in white shorts when I first met him, in later days when he visited Trivandrum or any other space centre, he always wore white khadi kurta pyjamas paired with well-worn Kolhapuri chappals. He never seemed to carry a wallet and always turned to his PA or some other accompanying aide if he needed money. In his pocket he usually had a simple black felt pen and on his wrist he wore an Indian-made HMT watch. On very special occasions I have seen him dressed in a formal dark brown bandhgala coat worn over pants. Only then would he wear shoes.

Over the years Dr Sarabhai's casual attire became an ISRO trend. Even the scientists who had worked abroad and were used to dressing in suits and ties now switched over to casual bush shirts and pants. Wearing chappals to work became the norm in ISRO, and it seemed perfectly sensible to dress this way, particularly in the hot and humid climates of Thumba, Ahmedabad and Bombay.

Sarabhai had an excellent equation with most of the leading scientists in this field in India and abroad. He also personally knew many leading politicians and business leaders. Since he came from an important industrialist family he was on a first-name basis with all those who mattered. And, since he had crucial roles to play in international scientific bodies, he was recognized by the heads of various international scientific agencies. This was vital because he could seek their assistance in solving many developmental issues.

When I met him for the first time in 1962, he must have been just forty-three years old. But he had a kind of aura of achievement around him already. He came from a family of industrialists and over the years he had helped set up a number of industries in Baroda and Bombay. He had created and fostered the Ahmedabad Textile Research Institute and the Physical Research Laboratory. He was instrumental in establishing the Indian Institute of Management at Ahmedabad. And yet he wore all these mantles with grace, never showing off or throwing his weight around.

People never failed to comment on the fact that he was 'born with a silver spoon in his mouth'. He might have had a privileged upbringing, but his parents and especially his mother made sure he had his feet firmly on the ground. He studied in the family school set up by his mother Sarala Devi Sarabhai. Later, he completed his degree from the Gujarat College in Ahmedabad and finally went to Cambridge. At the age of twenty he took his tripos in natural science from St. John's College. After he came back to India he joined the Indian Institute of Science and studied cosmic rays under Sir C.V. Raman.

There are many stories of young Vikram and his life in Bangalore in the early 1940s. Homi Bhabha, who was ten years his senior, also worked with Sir C.V. Raman at that time and the two became close friends. During a talk Professor Ramseshan gave at VSSC in Trivandrum on the twenty-fifth death anniversary of Vikram Sarabhai, he affectionately recounted some little-known incidents about his life. According to the professor, Vikram's father called him back to India when the Second World War broke out. He then took him to meet Sir C.V. Raman in Bangalore and sought a research position under him. Sir Raman asked the young Vikram if his father had dragged him there by the collar. Apparently Vikram answered, 'No sir, I told him I would return to India only if I could work with you!' Sir Raman was so pleased that he immediately took him on and offered him a stipend of Rs 30 a month.

Ramseshan said, 'I was never able to find out if Vikram took Raman's offer of Rs 30 per month, but his social activities would have cost him much more! Bhabha and he were seen almost every day at the West End Hotel and the clubs surrounded by beautiful women, much to the envy of all at the Indian Institute of Science.'

It was during those days that young Vikram met the beautiful dancer Mrinalini Swaminathan. She was the daughter of renowned barrister Dr Swaminathan, who was the principal of the Madras Law College, and Ammu, a freedom fighter and famous social worker. Mrinalini had trained in dance in Switzerland, Santinikethan, Kerala and the US before coming to Bangalore. They fell in love, got married and settled down in Malleswaram. Both of them were in their early twenties.

Sadly, theirs, it seems, was not a congenial marriage. Even though they had two children and stayed married to each other, there were many stories of Vikram Sarabhai's other liaisons. The most talked about of these was his long-standing relationship with Kamla Chaudhary for whom he is supposed to have set up the IIM at Ahmedabad. This controversial, much-discussed relationship was also whispered about in the corridors of TERLS. Was the great man really in love with another woman? And wasn't she his wife's close friend? We also got to know this beautiful and imperious woman as she often visited Thumba.

There were also many stories of Vikram Sarabhai's science experiments during his early years in Bangalore. One of his most important achievements was the building of complicated telescopes to detect cosmic rays, using only indigenous materials, as imported material was scarce during the war years. Cosmic rays continued to be his special area of interest. Once the Second World War was over, he went back to Cambridge to complete his research and got his doctoral degree.

But, of course, I did not have all this information about Dr Sarabhai in the mid-1960s. I was just a young man in my twenties. To me and to the rest of my equally young colleagues, he was like God. Our vibrant leader, whom we all loved, respected and looked up to. Vikram Sarabhai was like the central pillar of a big circus tent – the sole structure holding a rather diffuse set of units together. And we were the agile young artistes.

In Trivandrum, a visit by Dr Sarabhai was a momentous event eagerly anticipated by all of us. He had this gift of making each person feel very important and wanted. He listened to whatever proposals we put up with total attention and never discouraged us from experimenting. We would keenly await his visits to Thumba so we could show off what we had worked on. Then there were the important decisions that were taken during these visits. Space was still not a full-fledged government department. All our activities were under the aegis of DAE but the day-to-day control was with PRL, of which too Sarabhai was the director. Everything was informal. Take, for instance, the funding of projects. There was no formal budgeting. Most of the approvals for funding were taken on the spot. Sarabhai's loyal colleague and devotee S.R. Thakore usually wrote down the amounts sanctioned in a thick ledger, Bania-style! Sarabhai was always accompanied by a circle of colleagues from Ahmedabad, and he would confer with them before taking that on-the-spot decision. Chitnis, whom I had met on my very first visit to

Ahmedabad, was part of this inner circle. This quick granting of approval was possible also because the budget demands were minuscule compared to the astronomical sums needed today.

Sarabhai invariably stayed at the quaint Halcyon Castle at Kovalam belonging to the Travancore royal family. The castle on a cliff with a spectacular view had been converted into a small seaside hotel by the maharaja much before a five-star hotel was built near the same spot. Sarabhai chose to stay here because he loved to swim in the shallow, pristine Kovalam Bay.

Sarabhai's day started at five every morning with a swim in the calm waters of Kovalam. After a simple breakfast he would drive down to Thumba and Veli Hills. Then would follow a quick tour of all the new things the scientists had done since his last visit, usually a month earlier. He would watch exciting simulated tests of subsystems developed by various groups, inspect new buildings and new equipment, and carefully listen to mini-presentations by enthusiastic young engineers asking for more grants. Sarabhai would never turn down a request for a visit for he was well aware of the electrifying effect his presence had on the young teams.

The organization was in its formative stage and the R&D groups had not been clearly delineated. May be this was done deliberately so that there could be multiple proposals and different approaches for the same objective. This management strategy seemed to work very well at the initial stages when competition and rivalry between groups were actually encouraged to spark off innovation. Sarabhai would also directly interact with individuals who he thought had potential. Although this was greatly inspirational for the young person who was in focus, it did cause more than a little heartburn to the veterans who were used to the traditional hierarchical methods.

Kalam and I had a taste of this once in the mid-1960s when we got embroiled in what we would later laughingly refer to as 'The Great Corridor War'. Sarabhai would summon us often to PRL at Ahmedabad for major consultations or discussions. Kalam and I had made many such trips to PRL. Since we were two very junior engineers, we would travel all the way from Trivandrum by train through Madras Central and Bombay, taking two days each way.

This time too we reached PRL after a tiring journey. We had to wait for Sarabhai's arrival. As usual, we had to hang around in the corridors, as PRL had no specific space for visitors to sit. Sometimes, if we spotted colleagues we knew, we would chat for a while and they would ask us to come and sit with them. And we would hang around in their offices, as we really didn't consider ourselves visitors. PRL was a small organization and we knew practically everyone there.

On this occasion it took a little longer for Sarabhai to come and so our wait got extended. To this day I do not know what prompted him, but one of our colleagues, who had been chatting with us, suddenly complained to the local administration that we were generally disrupting the work because we were at a loose end. And so, unexpectedly, the administrative head came and shooed us out of the room.

She also told us we should not enter the rooms or disturb the work.

We were both furious. We had come there directly after a long and arduous journey from Trivandrum. We had also dropped our own important projects and taken time off from our busy schedules because Sarabhai had summoned us. We had been waiting for a couple of hours. To be bundled out now was the last straw.

Right there in that corridor we erupted. The normally soft-spoken Kalam was thoroughly incensed and so was I. We vented our anger on the administrative officer who was a fairly senior person. We said we would leave for Trivandrum immediately if we were not wanted. She told us not to be hasty and beat a retreat, not knowing what else to say.

But we were truly very junior engineers and neither of us had received any special recognition from Sarabhai at that time. So, the truth was, we could not really afford to leave, in spite of all our anger and frustration. Another senior person came and told us that Sarabhai was still caught up in a meeting. We were quite spent by now and stood leaning against the corridor walls, watching tiredly as some office assistants began moving furniture into a room adjoining the director's office.

Suddenly one of them came towards us. Our visitor's room was ready, he said, and would we please comfortably sit there until Sarabhai could see us! We were completely taken aback. We learned later that Sarabhai had heard about our outburst and its cause, and instead of getting angry with us, he had actually sympathized and got a waiting room readied so we could sit. When he finally met us he was as cordial and full of enthusiasm as usual, and all our anger and frustration melted away in a moment.

Sarabhai made it a point to know every employee by name, and this helped him to strike a personal rapport with each one of them. Everyone from a mali to a senior scientist felt he had a special relationship with Dr Sarabhai and therefore had to put up his best performance. He had his own way of making a young engineer feel very special. I remember an occasion when, as a junior engineer, I was travelling to Bombay from Trivandrum. I disembarked at Bombay and was getting into the waiting hall when I spotted Sarabhai surrounded by senior officials of DAE. They seemed to be in intense discussion.

To my great surprise and embarrassment, when he saw me arriving he simply left the group and hastened towards me as if I were a long-lost friend. He asked me about my trip and the progress of my work before requesting a senior official to see to it that I was dropped off at the guest house in the office car. I could see the puzzled expressions on some of the very senior persons he had left sitting. And, as for me, I felt very special that he had left them in mid-coversation to come and speak to me!

Once, when he visited Thumba in our very early days, he found that there was no technical library. We were sitting in the control centre in a big group as usual, discussing various amenities which we still needed. The question of a technical library came up.

Suddenly he turned to me and in his usual brisk manner said, 'Dan, why don't you prepare a proposal for a library with a proper budget. You can meet me at my Bombay office once it's ready.'

I got my report ready and flew to Bombay to meet him at his office at the Old Yacht Club. I was very nervous. This was the first time a major task of this nature had been entrusted to me. I waited with great trepidation. Would he be satisfied? There were already several senior scientists and officials waiting outside his office to see him. Would he have time to see me at all, I wondered. Suddenly his PA announced my name and I could see a couple of sour glances thrown my way. Some senior people had been waiting for quite a while.

I went in and presented my proposal, worried he would reject it. He just gave it one glance. 'Good!' he said. 'Just go ahead. And let me know if you need anything.'

That was all! I came out walking on air. I knew then that it was my bounden duty to implement the project immediately and to do a perfect job because Dr Sarabhai himself had entrusted me with it.

Sarabhai's monthly visit to Trivandrum would also attract a whole lot of visitors from his other areas of interest. Apart from those interested in discussing matters related to atomic energy with him, there were politicians, businessmen and even artistes. They would wait patiently for a chance to meet him. And he was always gracious with them, giving each one a patient hearing.

Lunch would always be a working one and technical issues would be thrashed out during this time. The return flights to Bombay from Trivandrum usually left in the afternoon, but Sarabhai would still be deep in discussion, much past the reporting time. But not to worry, since no flight would take off without him! Word would have gone to the airport chief and the plane would wait, passengers and all, for his arrival. I have known many occasions when, unable to complete his discussions, he would ask scientists to quickly buy a ticket to board the aircraft so that they could continue to talk with him during the flight. They would often take a return flight back to Trivandrum the same day, having completed the discussions in the plane and in the airport lounge!

On the days when he stayed back, he would work nonstop until well past midnight, continuously discussing the progress and problem areas with different groups who would be waiting, bleary-eyed, for their turn. Sarabhai, however, would be as fresh as ever, as he seemed to need very little sleep. And, no matter what time he retired in the night, he always got up at the crack of dawn for his swim. He loved south Indian food like sambhar, rasam, rice, idli, dosa, and also enjoyed Gujarati and Punjabi food. He particularly loved filter kaapi. Sarabhai was a strict vegetarian and never touched alcohol.

With his multiple responsibilities Sarabhai had to be constantly on the move within India and abroad. In those times before electronic ticketing I have seen Warrier, his PA, carrying a sheaf of air tickets, sometimes with alternate routes, covering weeks of travel. Of course, those were the days when Indian Airlines had a monopoly. He seemed to have no time for his family and perhaps that was responsible for the rumoured rifts in his marriage. Or was it the other way around? We never knew.

At the end of December 1971 Sarabhai was on one of his visits to Thumba. SSTC was fully functional in Veli Hills, with many of the proposed buildings and labs in place. Sarabhai had successfully persuaded the then railway minister to create a station at Veli so that employees could commute easily from the city.

A formal inauguration ceremony was arranged. K. Hanumanthaiah, the railway minister, wearing his typical Mysore turban, arrived at Thumba along with Sarabhai, who was dressed in a brown formal bandhgala for the occasion. Some of us noticed a hint of tiredness in Sarabhai which was untypical. Maybe he was overworked, we said, as we chatted amongst ourselves.

The inauguration ceremony went off well and thereafter he started his usual series of meetings with the engineers and scientists on the progress of various developmental programmers. Sarabhai's meetings normally spilled over to his hotel in the evenings. Once he left the Thumba area, we would all follow him in a cavalcade of cars. At the Halcyon Castle in Kovalam the meetings invariably stretched well into the night.

This time the plans for the development of the SLV and its various subsystems as well as the details of the constructions at SHAR were the leading topics of discussion. I remember the scene at the makeshift conference hall at the Halcyon Castle where we jostled with each other to present our plans. My project, which I needed to discuss with him, was the establishment of the radar tracking and telemetry systems at SHAR.

It was almost midnight of 29 December 1971 when some of us left for home. Sarabhai was still going strong. We knew that he hardly slept a few hours every day and would be up at 5 a.m. irrespective of when he went to bed the previous night. We learned later that he had promised the architect Charles Correa, who happened to be staying there, that he would join him for a dip in the sea the next morning at dawn.

I reached home around midnight and went to bed exhausted. At around 6 a.m. I was getting ready for an early start, when my phone rang. The person at the other end was Shankar, the PTI representative in Trivandrum. I had interacted with Shankar quite a few times during the launches and I thought he was ringing to ask about Dr Sarabhai's programme. I was totally unprepared for the devastating news he gave me. At first I thought it was some kind of a cruel joke.

He was frantically asking me if it was true that Dr Sarabhai has passed away. I was furious since I had seen Sarabhai hale and hearty hardly a few hours before. But before I could react my phone got entangled in a crossed line with a Delhi number which was hooked to Shankar's call. I could hear him instructing PTI Delhi to keep the news item ready.

'I will confirm it soon,' he said.

I put the phone down and stood there in a daze, unable to even react to my wife's anxious questions. The phone rang again. This time the call was from my PA. He gave me the same terrible news. He said my car was on its way to pick me up. A colleague got into the vehicle with me and we rushed to Kovalam.

Kovalam was little more than 12 km away. The road was bad but there was hardly any traffic. I had travelled that road hundreds of times during my seven-years' stay in Trivandrum. But that day the road seemed interminably long. The familiar coconut trees and thatched huts moved by in a blur.

At the gates of the hotel we saw groups of colleagues standing around. Everyone seemed in a daze. Our range doctor stood helplessly twiddling a stethoscope. He saw me and shook his head sadly. Our administrative officer spotted me and rushed up, saying, 'It's all over, Mr Dan. It's all over.'

We drove up the sloped drive and stopped at the portico. We could see the Chief Secretary of the Kerala government looking extremely agitated. He was accompanied by the police chief. Obviously Delhi had been notified and they had had instructions from the highest authorities to check out what happened.

I walked into the bedroom and saw the familiar and much-loved pyjama and kurta-clad form of Sarabhai lying on the bed. He seemed to be asleep. He wore an expression of peace – almost as if he knew he had completed his share of the tasks satisfactorily and handed them over to others to carry on.

I stood there for a few moments mourning my mentor. The muted sounds and bustle around me disappeared as I recalled our genial moments of interaction. I could almost imagine him jumping up and saying, 'Come on, Dan, there's work to be done. Now what do you have for me this time?'

Soon the entire Kerala cabinet descended on the hotel. Chief Minister Achutha Menon and his cabinet colleagues had a meeting on the spot. They seemed to be in touch with Delhi as well. The body was brought out and laid in the portico. The small crowd that had gathered there filed past, paying its respects.

The departure of the Indian Airlines flight leaving for Bombay was delayed by a few hours and the body was taken in a procession to the airport. The flight had been held up many a time for Dr Sarabhai in the past – but this time it was tragically different.

By the time we reached the airport, a huge crowd of employees and others had built up around the runway. It was a tough call for the local police to control the crowd. Finally the coffin was loaded on to the Boeing 737 and the flight left for Bombay en route to Ahmedabad.

Almost everyone including Murthy left for Ahmedabad. I was the most senior person left in charge of a desolate range in Trivandrum. And, before I knew it, I had plunged into another crisis, which left me totally shaken.

8

Turbulent Times

Some months earlier we had decided to try placing some concrete tetrapods at two ends of the Thumba beach in order to ensure proper range safety along the coast. This was to prevent people from walking back and forth particularly during launches. The local fishermen had already protested, saying this would infringe on their freedom. However, as an experimental measure it had been decided to place one or two tetrapods anyway to see whether they would stay in position or get washed away. Unfortunately the day chosen for this much in advance coincided with the day on which Dr Sarabhai's last rites were being performed in Ahmedabad.

The tetrapod placement was to be carried out under the security provided by the small Central Industrial Security Force (CISF) contingent which had just been posted at Thumba. TERLS was one of the first organizations to induct the newly created CISF and this contingent was still new to the job.

It was a holiday and I was at home when I received an urgent call. It was the assistant commandant of the CISF. He said there had been some confrontation with the fishermen who had obstructed the operation. They had assembled in large numbers and started attacking the security forces, he told me. The CISF had panicked and called the police. The police contingent arrived and found a big crowd of militant fishermen armed with stones and sticks. They had been forced to resort to firing and one young man was killed.

Already reeling under the shock of my mentor's death, I now had a new problem to deal with, something unprecedented. I called for a vehicle and rushed to the spot. The beach had already been cleared and various security people including the police commissioner and the CISF commandant were discussing what to do next.

I had never faced such a situation before. I had lived a fairly cocooned life so far, interacting with my colleagues only on technical matters. Now I was suddenly faced with a very human situation which had many nuances. The family of the young boy who was killed was distraught. The police said it was an accident. The fisherfolk were on the warpath. And I couldn't even consult any of my seniors on what should be done next.

Over the next couple of days I spoke to Murthy and we took the decision to halt the tetrapod experiment. The brother of the fisherman who was killed was promised a job at ISRO. A case had been lodged and a judicial enquiry ordered which dragged on for many months. More importantly, various politicians who had been waiting like hawks in the wings began circling in. So far our little rocket station had functioned without political interference. In a way, this was a coming-of-age for the organization. Things were never the same again.

Sarabhai's death was so sudden and shocking that we did not know what hit us. The long-term programmes of the space organization were just being formulated. We were still getting our funding sorted out, we were transitioning. And at this very crucial time we were left leaderless. Sarabhai had not named a second in command or even groomed a successor.

Adding to the confusion, Prime Minister Indira Gandhi's office summoned the persons they presumed were senior scientists and engineers to Delhi for discussions on the future course of action. This caused plenty of heartburn. Dr Sarabhai had not frozen the hierarchical structure, and there were many unclosed chains of command peopled by scientists and engineers of equal seniority. Maybe we needed a good leader from outside the organization who would be acceptable to all of us. But would new leaders be appointed arbitrarily without consulting all of us? Some of the senior scientists sent off telegrams to Delhi signed by a number of Trivandrum employees.

But obviously the PM had some sane advisors. She decided to nominate the brilliant and stylish Caltech-trained aeronautical engineer, Professor Satish Dhawan, as the person to carry forward the torch. Professor Dhawan was an experienced man with a proven track record. However, he told Mrs Gandhi he could not join immediately as he was committed to Caltech for a couple more months. He also had some other stipulations. He would join only if he could simultaneously continue as the director of the Indian Institute of Science (IISc) in Bangalore and he also wanted to locate the space department's HQ in Bangalore.

Indira Gandhi agreed to everything. She requested the eminent physicist Professor M.G.K. Menon to hold the fort until Dhawan could take over. Menon functioned as chairman of ISRO from January to September 1972.

Perhaps by the late 1960s Sarabhai himself had thought of a successor for the space programme. Perhaps he had identified Dhawan whom he had inducted as a member of the Atomic Energy Commission, which was also looking after space. And perhaps that was why Prime Minister Indira Gandhi had summoned him from Caltech to take over the apace activities. Or so the office gossip went. H.N. Sethna was appointed chairman of the Atomic Energy Commission, which had also become leaderless after Dr Sarabhai's death. Had he also been informally anointed by Sarabhai before his death? Thumba was abuzz with speculation.

Menon, our interim chairman, was quite well known in Thumba as he was a frequent visitor there along with Sarabhai. He was already chairman of the Electronics Commission of India and director of the Tata Institute of Fundamental Research (TIFR). His new task was a tough one because he had to deal with an abruptly orphaned organization which consisted of disparate elements that were, until then, independently reporting to Sarabhai. He had to urgently pick up the pieces and try to form a coherent organizational structure, as well as articulate some well-defined programme guidelines.

M.G.K. Menon more than lived up to the task thrust upon him. He brought in important and major structural changes in the organization in consultation with Dhawan. One of his first decisions was to relocate the project for building indigenous satellites to Bangalore under U.R. Rao. This was a practical move from a technical point of view since the humid coastal climate of Trivandrum could play havoc with the delicate electronic parts used in building satellites. Besides, Bangalore also had better support infrastructure from established organizations such as HAL and Bharat Electronics Limited (BEL) and some other private electronic industries. This move, however, created a huge outcry in Trivandrum as it was seen as an attempt to shift projects out of Kerala. But Menon managed to assuage these fears and the shift was made relatively painlessly. Trivandrum then became the centre for launch vehicle development activities.

The eminent metallurgist Brahm Prakash was appointed director of SSTC. This was a crucial decision since SSTC was, until then, directly handled by Sarabhai, with a group of persons, all of equal seniority, reporting directly to him. Menon rightly decided that Brahm Prakash was a scientist with proven ability who was also senior in age and experience, and would be acceptable to all of us. Subsequently Professor Yash Pal was moved from TIFR to take over as the director of the Space Applications Centre (SAC), which was a consolidation of various departmental units in Ahmedabad.

Brahm Prakash set about similarly consolidating the various units in Trivandrum. Soon, TERLS, SSTC, RFF and RPP were combined into what is now known as the Vikram

Sarabhai Space Centre (VSSC). Brahm Prakash became its first director. S.V. Kulkarni, a retired bureaucrat from DAE, was appointed the controller of administration of VSSC.

Dhawan returned to India after his stint at Caltech and assumed charge as chairman, ISRO, by the end of 1972. I can never forget the day of Dhawan's first visit to Thumba. We were accustomed to Sarabhai's visits which often resembled some kind of endless durbar – the whole place would be abuzz with activity and everyone milled around him, trying to capture the chairman's attention. We did not know what to expect of the new chairman.

That day all of us waited with great anticipation for this professor about whom we had heard so much. We wanted to flood him with our reports and proposals. I arrived at the airport early and, as was usual in those innocent pre-hijacking days, walked straight on to the tarmac. I was surprised to see our resplendently turned out CISF men lined up almost up to the bottom step of the mobile staircase of the aircraft. In an attempt to impress the chairman, Kulkarni had ordered our entire CISF force to form a ceremonial guard of honour to receive Dhawan at the airport.

I will never forget Dhawan's expression of shock and surprise when he got down from the aircraft along with the other passengers. At first he thought the guard of honour was for some other visiting VIP. And then he realized it was for him and not for some top military brass! He was taken ceremoniously by a special vehicle to Thumba. He had motorcycle outriders and a pilot car, followed by a procession of official cars. By the time we reached, I could see his surprise had turned into annoyance. Having been an academic all his life, he obviously disapproved of the pomp and ceremony.

At Thumba he was introduced to the senior officials who took him on a round of visits to some of the laboratories and gave him a presentation of the ongoing activities. It was now beyond working hours, but the milling crowd of scientists and engineers was still around him. We were all used to Sarabhai's style and we assumed the new chairman would carry on working through the evening, until midnight and beyond.

Suddenly Dhawan looked around. 'Why are you all still here?' he asked. 'Isn't it time for you to go home?'

We all stopped in our tracks! Go home? So early? It was unthinkable. How could we leave the chairman and go home at this time? But Dhawan was adamant. He gently told us to take a break and come back refreshed the next day! It took us time before to get adjusted to this new style of functioning. This was far more practical – a systematic and level-headed style. We had got used to bursts of intense and unbroken activity followed by lull periods, and we almost did not know how to cope with this.

Sarabhai's management style was that of a patriarch dealing with a small well-knit family. It was a kind of monolithic structure and Sarabhai operated on a one-to-one basis. There were no formal systems in place, with parallel technical teams operating. Sometimes they would work on the same systems without any coordination. This was fine while the organization was just building up. The long-term goals had not yet been carefully defined and government funding was yet to come in. So we could, in a sense, take our own time.

But now the time had come to introduce formalized management structures with clear accountability. The informal and casual style of management had to change if government funding and public accountability were to be brought in. The budget demands were becoming larger by the day. Accountability to the Parliament and to the public for the money spent would soon become vital. We would need to begin showing results. Sarabhai had probably realized all this and begun work on putting the systems in place. But Sarabhai, the iconic father figure, had passed away at this very crucial juncture. And now, Dhawan the academic had brought in a totally new style of functioning.

His first task was to bring some order into the widely dispersed teams by integrating them and defining their individual roles and collective responsibilities. This he did by forming programme-based centres with undisputed leadership. He also arranged for a national-level review of the long-term tasks of ISRO in association with internal and external experts. The agencies which would be the ultimate users of our programmes were also included in the dialogue. The recommendations and action items of this exercise were used to formulate demands for grants from the government.

Dhawan's style of management was quite businesslike. He followed the HQ type of structure by hiring management-educated and experienced young men as shadow teams. They would function from the HQ and make a technical and budgetary analysis of each programme. They would provide him with daily feedback on the progress and indicate problem areas. Dhawan also introduced an elaborate annual budget exercise. Senior personnel from all the centres were assembled at HQ. The directors and project managers presented their proposals in open forums, and could be grilled by everyone present. This ensured there was clarity and no duplication. Meanwhile, the band of young men from HQ whom we had nicknamed the Blue-eyed Boys would take frantic notes and ask tough questions.

The change in style was difficult to deal with at first. But soon we realized that this kind of change was inevitable, given the increasing complexity and size of the budgets involved. The scrutiny became more rigorous. Our new chairman was a dignified man with great intellectual honesty. He encouraged honest criticism and was quick to recognize merit. Sarabhai's style was fine when the structure was loose and still evolving. But now we needed to freeze things and get on to execution mode. Dhawan exactly fitted the role, with his systematic approach and no-nonsense style.

Dhawan was very particular that local industry and academia should be associated with the programmes. He felt there should be a two-way dissemination and absorption of expertise. So he inducted organizations like HAL, HMT and BEL and institutions like IISc and government research laboratories to partner ISRO. Under the Respond programme small grants were given to various research organizations to undertake specific projects for space research.

Meanwhile, trade unions had become a force to reckon with inside ISRO. During the last years of the 1960s manpower had increased at a rapid pace. There was a significant increase in the number of scientists and engineers as well as technicians and tradesmen. We functioned in Kerala, the land of vibrant trade unions. So by the early 1970s a variety of labour unions, of different hues, began to emerge. The competition between them led to frequent shows of strength and no single body was able to have a sustained dialogue with the management.

I clearly remember the first time we had a major problem, soon after Brahm Prakash took over. He was working in his chamber when a big group of employees rushed into his office. Some of them started banging on his door and shouting slogans, and the rest sat down on the corridors outside his office.

I got a frantic call from his PA. I rushed out to find some of my senior colleagues also headed in the same direction. The corridors outside his office were filled with slogan-shouting men. This was the first time I had actually faced a dharna. Little did I know then how familiar this scene would become over the years.

They were all known faces – people with whom we worked on a day-to-day basis. But suddenly they all seemed to have turned hostile. It was a new and frightening experience. They made way for us and allowed us to get into Dr Brahm Prakash's chamber, but it was a trap! No one was allowed to get out again, unless their demands were met. We did not even know what their demands were and the din outside was increasing in tempo.

We had until then never heard of the term 'gherao' and this was our first experience of it. It lasted for more than four hours. None of us could get out. In those days there was no attached toilet in the director's office and we were not allowed to go to the common toilet or get a bite to eat or even a drink of water.

We started making frantic calls to the police and the chief minister's office for help. Finally it arrived in the form of a small contingent of Reserve Police led by C. Subrahmanyan, a young and smart IPS officer. He wasted no time in dispersing the crowd and restoring some semblance of order.

This, however, was just the beginning. Soon hartals and gheraos became a part of our work routine. For some time, in the beginning, there was a general atmosphere of disorder. Not much work could be done. The problem was compounded by the rivalries between the different unions affiliated to a variety of political parties. Dhawan was quite ruthless when it came to cleaning up undesirable and obstructive elements. But he was also quick to realize that organized labour had to be respected and encouraged to cooperate with the management to successfully achieve the objectives of the organization. So he introduced the Joint Consultative Machinery (JCM).

The next few years saw a lot of changes within the organization. H.G.S. Murthy left TERLS to join the UN and I was made the range director. In addition, Brahm Prakash entrusted me with the task of organizing a systems reliability group in VSSC. The emphasis shifted from sounding rockets to the development of a satellite launch vehicle capability and we needed a larger launch base. Kalam, Easwaradas and I were given larger tasks in tune with the changed objectives.

As the range director of TERLS, I suddenly found myself in total command of the little launching station I had helped to establish. Initially it was a challenging task as the sounding rocket programme was going on at a brisk pace and I had to take care of all the administrative issues involved. But soon it became obvious that the era of bigger rockets and satellites had arrived, and Thumba's importance would ebb as the activities shifted to Sriharikota.

It was at this point of time that Dr Brahm Prakash asked me to shift to SSTC on Veli Hills and set up a reliability and quality assurance group. Brahm Prakash integrated all the quality, testing and reliability activities in Trivandrum and formed the systems reliability group, appointing me its group director. This group was the first full-time and independent quality agency in ISRO, set up to overview the R&QA activities of products, subsystems, procedures and protocols.

The SLV programme began taking shape under Kalam while the Rohini satellite team was functioning in Bangalore under U.R. Rao. Y.J. Rao was in charge of the development of SHAR and Yash Pal of SAC. In the last years of the 1970s, everything was geared towards conducting the first experimental launch of SLV-3 with the Rohini satellite as the payload.

Meanwhile, Dhawan asked me to look at ISRO-wide reliability procedures, particularly with reference to inter-centre projects. And thus was born the ISRO Reliability team, ISREL, a core group at the ISRO HQ in Bangalore. ISREL played a key role in integrating the reliability activities of various ISRO centres, and evolving common standards and protocols. Soon, all the centres of ISRO set up their own reliability organizations. The consistent and dramatic successes which brought fame to ISRO nationally and internationally owe a lot to this silent and dedicated group who stayed away from the limelight and evolved their own methodology of work ethics.

An important aspect of this discipline was the non-applicability of methods and practices of western countries and organizations like NASA or ESA; these would not work here because India did not have the industrial, scientific and military base those countries had. Therefore ISRO had to develop its own methods and protocols. The R&QA teams always had to do a bit of 'hand-holding' of the development groups and sometimes even had to resort to 'concurrent development and qualification' to hasten schedules.

By the mid-1970s I was sitting in a spacious air-conditioned office on the eighth floor of the SSTC building on Veli Hills. I had a view of the sea and Veli Lake on one side and hills on the other. Often, as I looked out at the campus sprawled around me – at the beautiful buildings, the trees, the gardens, the fleets of buses, the cars whizzing busily up and down – I would think of those days when there were no roads and even the payload had to be carried to the pad on a bicycle. I would remember our sole motorized vehicle – a van that lay idle until our roads came up.

Tough as those days were, there was a certain warmth about them, a family-like atmosphere which was now sadly gone forever. Sarabhai was the rare leader who had inspired total dedication in us. We had put into the building of

Thumba the kind of physical, emotional and mental energy one normally invested in personal matters. Every one of our little achievements was an achievement for the Thumba family; every little setback was a personal one.

I would remember our first taste of luxury when we moved into the air-conditioned control centre by the sea – never mind that the air conditioning was really meant for the equipment and not for us! At that time I missed the pigeons in the church building, but I had a cubicle to myself and a steno to help me. I felt then that it was big step forward. Later, when Murthy left and I moved into his office, I felt I was actually afloat in the sea as the waves washed up on all sides of that beautiful little room. By then I had bought my own car and would drive up to the range where we had a couple of vehicles to transport us from point to point.

Our luxury had come in little spurts – a good launcher, air-conditioned assembly buildings, a canteen, bus services… From those small roots had grown this vast organization which had spread all over the country. Of course in the 1970s and '80s ISRO was nowhere as large as it is now.

But to us it already seemed enormous. Because of the vastness and complex nature of the operations there could be no personal involvement. Gone were the days when we all assembled the rocket, carried it personally to the launch pad, checked out the systems, went back, pressed the button and received the telemetry signals. We had reached the era of SLV and PSLV launches. The kind of technical input required, the coordination involved between various centres, and the sheer enormity of the tasks precluded such involvement. We now sat in our separate plush air-conditioned offices, each one of us absorbed in our own commitments and projects.

ISRO, as an entity, was formed in 1969 just before the passing away of Sarabhai. But the ISRO we know today began to take shape only after Dhawan took charge. Four distinct geographical areas now emerged: Trivandrum, Bangalore, Sriharikota and Ahmedabad. They were all fed with people from the mother centre at Trivandrum. Specific sub-projects were defined in various centres for the launch vehicle and satellite development. There were fixed budgets and time schedules.

Our old group had now spread out. We had different responsibilities and different destinies. Buddy (Ramakrishna Rao), whose path had run almost parallel to mine, was made the head of the electronics division, looking after the development of on-board electronic subsystems. Sadly, immediately after the death of Sarabhai, during the brief tenure of M.G.K. Menon as chairman, Buddy was accused of spying and misusing government equipment, and was suspended. The equipment in question was a high power HAM radio set which had been sent to ISRO along with the telemetry trailer. He had taken the radio set home for his private use. Buddy was moved to ISRO HQ and he engaged in lengthy litigation with the organization. He had his ups and downs until the case was finally dismissed. He passed away after a few years, reportedly of a heart attack.

After the initial years of TERLS Prakash Rao went back to PRL to do his PhD under U.R. Rao and worked abroad for some time before returning to join ISRO Satellite Centre

(ISAC). Kale continued in PRL doing ISRO work. He joined SAC when it was formed and was involved with the Satellite Instructional Television Experiment (SITE) programme. Easwaradas was put in charge of the rocket assembly and launching group at TERLS. After a couple of years, he took over the RFF and then moved on to become the deputy director of the mechanical facility of VSSC. Kalam, who was in charge of range safety and impact prediction in the initial days of TERLS, later became the head of the range engineering division. Dhawan then asked him to head the SLV-3 satellite launch vehicle project. Kalam got his first vehicle on the launch pad by the late 1970s.

By then the satellite launch vehicle programme had started in earnest and Sriharikota was already being developed as the launch site. Detailed project reports were prepared for the various subsystems. One of the ground-based subsystems was the radar tracking facility to be established in the launch base and other downrange stations. I was designated the project manager for this activity.

9

Streamlining

In June 1972, soon after Dhawan took over, the Department of Space and the policy body Space Commission were born. The first task was to make an integral entity of the various units in Thumba and Veli so that all energies could be channelized into achieving the objectives set out in the Decade Profile, which had been spelt out by Sarabhai in 1970. Centralized administration was brought in to avoid duplication and wastage.

The next important task was to impart momentum to the SLV project. During the last days of Sarabhai's leadership a fairly comprehensive definition of the subsystems and facilities required for the project had been compiled. Most of us pioneers were involved with the project during its definition stage and we would periodically give him our updates and progress reports. This happened until the very last night before he died.

During this phase, Y.J. Rao was the launch vehicle coordinator, Gowarikar was responsible for the first stage, Kurup for the second Muthunayagam for the third and

Setting up a special camera before a sounding rocket launch at the Wallops Station of NASA, Virginia. The author is second from right (1963).

Aravamudan (right) with Ramakrishna Rao operating a telemetry station at NASA (1963).

The early pioneers at the Wallops Launch Station of NASA, Virginia.
(From left to right) Aravamudan, A.P.J. Abdul Kalam, Murthy, Ramakrishna Rao and Easwaradas.

Aravamudan (extreme right) with the Tracking Radar equipment being readied for dispatch to India (1963).

The author (third from right) with the telemetry ground station he helped build at NASA near Washington, DC (1963).

A Nike apache test rocket launched from TERLS (1963).

The Church of Mary Magdalene in Thumba where the space programme started.

Aravamudan (in vest) and A.P.J. Abdul Kalam preparing a payload inside the church building in Thumba, Kerala (1964).

(From left to right) Aravamudan, E.V. Chitnis, S.C. Gupta and M.K. Mukherji with Sarabhai looking at development plans (mid-1960s).

Aravamudan with A.P.J. Abdul Kalam and D. Easwaradas during a meeting (mid-1960s).

During a sounding rocket discussion at TERLS in the mid-1960s. Aravamudan is seated at the centre. Two of the participants, U.R. Rao (seated extreme left) and G. Madhavan Nair (standing third from right), later became chairmen of ISRO. A.P.J. Abdul Kalam (seated second from right) became the President of India after about forty years!

Aravamudan and G. Madhavan Nair (mid-1960s).

Aravamudan demonstrating an optical radar acquisition device developed by him to the then scientific advisor to the defence minister (late 1960s).

RH 75 take-off (late 1960s).

Indira Gandhi dedicating TERLS to the United Nations in 1968.
Sarabhai is standing second from left.

Aravamudan explaining a ground tracking system at TERLS to
Sarabhai and a group of visitors.

Aravamudan with Sarabhai looking at a piece of moon rock brought by Armstrong and displayed in Trivandrum (1969).

THUMBA EQUATORIAL ROCKET LAUNCHING STATION
POST BOX NO. 35
TRIVANDRUM-1.
(INDIA)

TELEPHONES :
8351 to 8358.

March 20, 1970

MEMORANDUM

Shri R. Aravamudan, Head, Ground Support Division, Thumba Equatorial Rocket Launching Station (TERLS), is being deputed to West Germany, France, England, French Space Center in French Guiana (South America), NASA Installations at Washington DC, Cape Kennedy, Wallops Station, Houston, Huntsville and Dallas etc., in United States, Hawai to visit NASA Tracking Station, Australia to visit Satellite Launching Station, and NASA Tracking Station and to Japan to visit Kagoshima Satellite Launching Station/Center, from 12th April to 29th May, 1970. He will have technical discussions with engineers and scientists at various space centres in these countries and other institutions regarding the Indian Satellite Programme and connected matters. His itinerary is enclosed. This work is of very urgent nature for the planning and progress of the scientific satellite launching programme of Indian Space Research Organization (ISRO).

His economy class airfare Bombay/Zurich/Munich/Paris/London/Cayenne/Washington DC/Orlando/Miami/Huntsville/Houston/Dallas/Minneapolis/Los Angles/Sydney/Hawai/Tokyo/Calcutta/Madras/Trivandrum plus living expenses abroad will be paid by TERLS. In addition, he will also be paid incidental expenses and internal travel by TERLS.

(Vikram A. Sarabhai)
Chairman, ISRO

Encl: As above

Shri R. Aravamudan,
Head, Ground Support Division,
TERLS.

cc: Director TERLS
Admin.Officer PRL.

A deputation order signed by Sarabhai which enabled Aravamudan to visit some of the leading space stations in the world (1970).

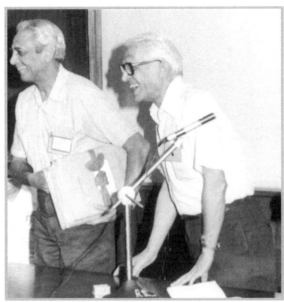

Satish Dhawan and
Brahmpakash in a lighter
moment (mid-1970s).

Aravamudan explaining details of a trajectory plotter to Satish Dhawan at
Thumba (mid-1970s).

Aravamudan explaining the Thumba layout to the then President of India, Fakhruddin Ali Ahmed. Satish Dhawan is to his left (mid-1970s).

Aravamudan receiving the then Prime Minister Morarji Desai at a static test stand in Thumba (1977).

ISRO

A.P.J. Abdul Kalam, Satish Dhawan and S. Srinivasan inspecting the first SLV vehicle under assembly (1979).

ISRO

S.C. Gupta explaining some precision payload components to Raja Ramanna. To his right are Vasanth Gowariker, Aravamudan and young S. Radhakrishnan, who later became chairman of ISRO (1970s).

ISRO

Indira Gandhi flanked by Vasanth Gowariker and Satish Dhawan after a successful SLV launch (1980).

A rare picture of the pioneers who developed the first Launch Vehicle. (Seated from left to right) Muthunayagam, S.C. Gupta, Gowarikar, A.P.J. Abdul Kalam, Dhawan, Brahmaprakash, Kurup, Easwara Das and Aravamudan.
(Standing in first row, from left to right) T. Sriram, Anantharam, Vedachalam, V. Sudhakar, B.C. Sarkar, Sudhakara Rao, M.A. Majeed, Namboodiri, G. Madhavan Nair, V.P. Kulkarni, D.S. Rane and S. Ramnath.
(Standing in second row, from left to right) B.C. Pillai, T. Pillai, C.R. Sathya, Sivathanu Pillai, Sreedharan Dhas, U.S. Singh, M.S.R. Dev, V.P. Sandlas, Sasikumar, S. Srinivasan, Sundararajan, M.C. Mathur, Rajaram Nagappa, Bhute and Soupramaniane.

Rajiv Gandhi at Sriharikota for an ASLV launch. He is accompanied by the Andhra CM, N.T. Rama Rao, K. Radhakrishnan (who years later became chairman of ISRO) and the then chairman U.R. Rao. The launch was a failure (1987).

At the PM's Office, the then Chairman Kasturirangan explaining a successful launch. Aravamudan who was the then Director of the satellite centre is to his left (1995–96).

In front of an INSAT satellite being assembled in the clean room at ISAC Bangalore (1996-97).

Old friends Aravamudan, Gita and President A.P.J. Abdul Kalam reliving Trivandrum days over a private dinner at Rashtrapati Bhawan (2007).

Enjoying a joke
with President
Kalam at the
Rashtrapati Bhawan
gardens (2007).

Aravamudan and his wife Gita (second and third from the right) at the PSLV
launch pad before the take-off of the Mars Orbiter Mission (2013).

The GSLV rocket taking
off from Sriharikota
(January 2014).

Aravamudan receiving the outstanding achievement award for contributions to ISRO from U.R. Rao (2014).

A panoramic view of a GSLV in the launch pad (August 2015).

A panoramic view of the PSLV launch pad (September 2016).

Kalam for the fourth. Ramakrishna Rao was in charge of
telemetry and I was in charge of tracking. Gupta was defining
the control and guidance package, Mukherjee the heat shield
and Amba Rao the launcher. Madhavan Nair was in charge
of telecommand and U.R. Rao the satellite. Each of us had
one-to-one conversations with Sarabhai regularly on progress
in our assigned areas.

So, there were quite a few competent people who could
take on the overall leadership role in the implementation of
the SLV-3 project. After careful consideration, the choice
fell on Kalam, who had an aeronautics background and
some experience in running a project. He was also known
for 'getting things done'. The project was also formally
sanctioned, with an exclusive group formed to manage it.
Funds were allocated with a defined time frame for execution.
The government sanction was for Rs 20 crores with a foreign
exchange component of Rs 6 crores. The first suborbital test
flight was to be completed by 1976 and the first orbital flight
by 1978.

Kalam roped in many Indian industries, both from the
public and private sectors, for fabrication as well as supply
of raw materials. The ISRO groups had a head start since
they had already started work on the design of solid rocket
motors and the associated hardware. The project had to do
an acceptance test of all the subsystems developed by various
agencies before integrating into the vehicle. Some of them,
like control and guidance packages, onboard telemetry
systems, tracking transponders and telecommand packages,
had to be flown in sounding rockets to prove their flight-

worthiness. In fact, the RH 560 sounding rocket developed by ISRO came in handy to test the control package and the algorithms involved.

On the labour front we continued to have problems. The JCM finally injected a degree of order into the dialogue between the parties. But, by the time we reached this stage, a couple of precious years had been wasted. Meanwhile, there was another area of concern that needed to be addressed immediately. The employees' wage structure had to be normalized taking into consideration each individual's qualification and experience.

In the initial years, employees were inducted into the organization from various sources and at various times on different terms. There was thus a wide range of salaries and wages for persons with the same qualification and experience. And these persons had to work together. This led to a lot of heartache and dissatisfaction. And so committees to address the issue of normalization were formed. We slogged over this for years, working overtime to define formulas which could be applied for rectifying the anomalies. We knew the solutions could never be watertight but we did our best.

This took up a considerable portion of the attention of the scientific and technical staff, delaying progress in the important development tasks set out. In order to try and balance both, we often worked on these tasks late at night, moving from centre to centre to understand the unique problems. It took about three to four years for the dust to settle on these issues and we were freed once more to tackle the technical tasks at hand.

One rather prolonged strike in 1978 was over an X-ray unit in RFF which the employees claimed was causing a wide set of problems ranging from impotency to hair loss. They refused to stay in the building whenever the unit was turned on. When the management decided to take action against this rather unscientific behaviour, senior engineers were gheraoed. The police contingent which came to their rescue was stoned. And when Brahm Prakash initiated action against the ringleaders, the problems only increased. There were more gheraos and even the bus drivers went on strike, creating major transport problems.

The X-ray unit was only a flashpoint. There was a general feeling of insecurity on the part of the workers about many of the major activities moving out of Trivandrum. Because of this they would not allow any equipment to be moved from one centre to another. For example, when an unused horizontal boring machine was to be shifted from the RFF to Sriharikota for the SLV project they prevented it. As a result the project got delayed by almost a year. It was only moved after a year because of the intervention of the then prime minister, Morarji Desai.

In 1978 the trade union activities of VSSC were at their peak and there were endless agitations. A.K. Antony was the chief minister of the Congress-led state government. VSSC director Brahm Prakash had been gheraoed over the machine tool incident. It was under these circumstances that Morarji Desai decided to visit us at Trivandrum.

Elaborate arrangements were made for the visit. Chairman Satish Dhawan wanted to showcase ISRO for the prime minister. We had chalked out a half-day programme. The PM was to be given a general briefing followed by a visit to the laboratories and the Thumba launch base. A static testing of a small rocket and the launch of a Rohini rocket were also scheduled.

Desai reached Veli Hills in the morning. All the senior engineers were lined up to greet him on arrival. I shook hands with him and as he passed me I got a very strong whiff of garlic! Dhawan gave him a complete presentation of the activities of ISRO. He was, after all, the minister in charge of space and this was his maiden visit. After a tour of the Veli laboratories he was driven down the hill to TERLS where the static firing of a small rocket was scheduled. I received him, as I was in charge of TERLS and the static testing unit.

A brief countdown was in progress for the firing when suddenly J.T. George, who was supervising the test, came running to me and whispered that there was something wrong with the firing circuit. He said it would take a while to rectify the problem and he did not want the PM to be delayed. I informed Dhawan who told the PM of the delay and suggested that we proceed to the next item in the visit. Morarji thought for a second and insisted on waiting. It took some effort on the part of Dhawan to convince him that anyway an actual launch was scheduled and so we could give the static test a miss.

A small pandal had been erected near the control centre along the beach where the VIPs were seated to witness the launching. Since I was the range director, I sat next to him and explained the finer points of the launch. The rocket to be fired was a small RH-300 and at count zero it made an impressive take-off without any hitch, to my great relief!

I accompanied him from the viewing platform to the control centre. We were standing in the middle of the room and there was no one else except me within earshot. He muttered something.

I thought he was speaking to me. I went closer to him and said, 'Pardon?'

He looked at me quizzically and said again in a soft voice, almost as if he were talking to himself, 'Where are they and where are we!'

I didn't quite know what to make of this rather enigmatic aside but those were lines I have never forgotten. Before I could recover from this, he suddenly demanded to speak to the employees. This unscheduled demand sent everyone into a flutter. We had to quickly assemble the employees and rig up a public address system.

Morarji addressed the workers at length. He stressed the need for discipline and order, especially given the importance of the highly specialized nature of our work. He did not hide his unhappiness over the recent incidents of violent agitations by the workers and warned them that the large investments planned for space science and technology could be diverted if the situation continued. Although Morarji's visit took care of the immediate labour unrest, the unions had come to stay and we knew we had to strike a proper rapport if work had to go on smoothly.

The design, development and fabrication of the rocket stages progressed. The solid motors cast in separate segments were made in Trivandrum. The first and second stage rocket cases were made of high-strength steel called 15CDV6. This was initially imported. The third and fourth stages were made of lightweight, high-strength, fibre-reinforced plastic fabricated in-house.

Industries like the Walchandnagar Group, Larsen & Toubro, HAL and many others participated in the programme. In fact, one of the main achievements of ISRO during those days was the involvement of the country's industries, academic institutions and research laboratories in India's space programme. They in turn benefitted because working with such high technologies enhanced their own capacities. Dhawan firmly believed this was an essential element of ISRO's philosophy. He wanted the future fabrication work to be left to the industries so that ISRO could concentrate on essential R&D.

From the mid-1970s, work on the pre-flight qualification of the SLV-3 motors and other subsystems started. Rocket stages were submitted to static testing. Avionic packages were tested in the laboratory. After this some of the packages were tried out in sounding rockets like Centaures and RH-560s. Expert teams conducted reviews to bring out any concerns. Meanwhile, the Sriharikota complex was also gearing up with launch pads, control centres, range instrumentation and safety systems.

I led the team that developed the C-band tracking radar installed in Sriharikota. This radar was the first indigenously built one in the country. TIFR, Bhabha Atomic Research Centre (BARC) and Electronics Corporation of India

Limited (ECIL) partnered with the ISRO teams for this project. It was very clear from the outset that building an indigenous precision tracking radar from scratch was going to be an exacting task. Radar technology, being strategic in nature, was not available for love or money from other countries. So, I knew we would have to do it the hard way with help from other institutions in the country, including academic institutions that had some expertise.

Radar technology is quite complicated as it involves the entire gamut of engineering, including precision machining, microwave transmission and reception, digital technology, servo systems and data processing. The Radar Development Project (RDP) was born when Sarabhai was alive. He was the one who roped in TIFR, ECIL and of course BARC – he wanted the RDP to tap the experience of these institutions. But he was also very clear that the project management, final integration, testing and installation should be done by us. We also had to develop the special subsystems, which others could not do.

I took charge of the RDP and this was in addition to my other regular work. A dedicated team was recruited and as usual temporary workspace was found in the old church building for this activity. A wing was partially air-conditioned for use as a laboratory. My core team initially included E. Janardhanan, G. Viswanathan, K. Jayaraman, K. Rajagopal and K. Natarajan. They took responsibility for the development of the various subsystems and also coordinated with other agencies in the process. They in turn were joined by other engineers to assist them in their tasks. M.G.K.

Menon was then director of TIFR. Under his guidance the TIFR team helped us with building the transmitter receiver chains for the radar. R.V.S. Sitaram and V.P. Kodali from TIFR played key roles in these developments.

The progress was slow, since the subject of precision radar tracking was new and many of the specialized parts had to be imported with great difficulty. Being military hardware, there were restrictions on the sale of some of these components. It was only in the late 1970s that we finally got the subsystems ready. Dhawan helped us to streamline the process. A temporary shed for integrating the subsystems was erected in the TERLS area. A concrete tower was built for positioning the antenna system. Our first thrill came when we turned on the system and received reflected signals from the objects around!

However, making the system function as tracking radar was a totally different cup of tea. Quite a lot of tuning and trimming had to be done. The operators had to be trained to recognize and acquire moving targets. The radar system had to work in conjunction with rocket-borne transponders to extend the tracking range and accuracy. All this took some more time.

After the initial trials at Thumba the system was carefully dismantled and moved to Sriharikota, where it was installed in a specially constructed building. One more such system was built and installed at SHAR. By 1979, the radar facility at SHAR was ready, well in time for the first experimental launch of our first indigenous launch vehicle, the SLV-3.

10

SLV: Our First Homegrown Launch Vehicle

Finally D-day arrived on 10 August 1979, a good five years after the date that Sarabhai had originally proposed. The SLV 3 was assembled for flight on the pad.

Kalam used to define the very act of bringing the assembled vehicle on to the launch pad as '50 per cent success'. He would go on to assign success percentages to various events, like the take-off, first-stage function, second-stage function and so on till the actual injection into orbit of the satellite.

The launch was scheduled for the early morning on 10 August 1979. And a few minutes after the vehicle took off, it crashed into the Bay of Bengal. Our first attempt at launching a satellite launch vehicle was unsuccessful.

Kalam would often say a noble leader would take the onus of failure on himself and give the credit for success to his subordinates. And now this was precisely what Dhawan did. He never once blamed Kalam or his team for the failure during the press conferences which followed. The media was not so aggressive in those days. But this was a landmark event and they were at the gates of SHAR, clamouring to know what had happened. Dhawan, who was very wary of the press, did not allow them in. He knew that the success of the mission at this stage was dicey. He also feared that undue publicity would be counterproductive.

We were all very disappointed. Kalam was particularly depressed although he knew, as we all did, that failures were quite common in the rocket business the world over. Dhawan and Brahm Prakash were very supportive. They urged everyone not to give up and to find out what went wrong and fix it. On analysis, it was found that the loss of control was due to the failure of the reaction control thruster system – an undetected leak had drained it of the control fluids. We put our heads down and set to work on another attempt.

Brahm Prakash, who headed VSSC during the years leading to the first attempted launch of SLV-3, retired in 1979. However, he continued as a member of the Space Commission. The task of seeing the SLV-3 project through and steering VSSC now fell on Vasanth Gowariker. We had all got used to the gentle and benevolent presence of Brahm Prakash who was almost a father figure both in age and stature. It took us a little while to restore the momentum of work.

The second SLV-3 launch was scheduled on 18 July 1980, almost a year after the first one. The payload was Rohini 1, a satellite weighing 40 kg. The mood was very tense this time around and not just because of the launch.

Sanjay Gandhi had died in a plane crash just a month ago even as we were putting the finishing touches to our vehicle. He had been trying out some acrobatic manoeuvres in his training aircraft. Delhi was in chaos as Indira Gandhi tried to come to terms with the loss. In Trivandrum and SHAR this had a trickledown effect, but we were determined to go ahead with our launch.

This time Dhawan had decided to allow Doordarshan to telecast the launch. The press was still not to be allowed inside until after the event. Since Doordarshan was not yet equipped to do a live telecast, some engineers from SAC had come up with an ingenious idea. They had tethered a huge balloon with a transponder halfway between SHAR and Madras. Gummidipoondi was the chosen location for the balloon which floated at a height of about 1 km above ground. A long strong cable secured it firmly to the ground. The distance as the crow flies from SHAR was about 80 km. Experts from TIFR's balloon facility at Hyderabad had been roped in for this project.

Yash Pal and I were to do the commentary in-house. Gita had also been invited to join us and ask questions from a layperson's point of view, and so she came with me from Trivandrum for this historic launch. We had left our small kids with Gita's parents in Bangalore. They were very excited at the prospect of seeing their parents live on TV. Bangalore still didn't have TV coverage in those days and so their grandparents had arranged to watch the launch at the house of a friend who had rigged up an extra-powerful antenna to catch Madras Doordarshan's telecast.

Everything was ready and the nervousness was palpable. The press at the gates had been baying for information for over three days. Inside, during one of the meetings, a senior scientist doodled loops and a crash on his notepad and remarked to his neighbour, 'As long as the rocket doesn't take the trajectory of Sanjay Gandhi's plane, we'll be fine!'

Yash Pal, Gita and I were rehearsing our questions the previous day when we heard some bad news. The blimp had flown off! This kind of balloon was usually used in events like carnivals which took place in areas where there was a benign breeze that created just a gentle oscillation. No one had accounted for the strong winds which roared through Gummidipoondi and wrenched the balloon off its tether. Nothing could be done about it as the launch was scheduled for the next day, at dawn. We decided to record the commentary and rush it to Madras by road.

The launch had its moment of nail-biting suspense. A few minutes prior to take-off the command was given to detach the umbilical cable from the rocket. There are two types of umbilical cables connecting the rocket to the ground. One set comes off automatically during take-off and the other set, which is much heavier, is detached remotely with an electrical command. The remote-controlled cable just refused to come off! For a few minutes no one knew what to do. Obviously the launch could not take place with a stuck cable so we had to call a 'Hold'.

The vehicle was fully armed and it was quite unsafe for anyone to venture near. The saviour of the day was a technician named Bapiah. He volunteered to climb up the launch tower and manually coax the cable off. The tower was around 60 ft high, which was about the same height as the rocket. We had no other option but to let him try, with the safety officials turning their backs for a short while. Bapiah quickly climbed the tower and gave the cable a hefty kick – and it mercifully came off! The rest, of course, is history. The flight was a maiden success – a milestone in ISRO's history.

And so on 18 July 1980, almost seventeen years after the first foreign Nike-Apache sounding rocket was launched from TERLS, a made-in-India rocket launched from Indian soil injected an Indian-made satellite into a 300 km by 900 km orbit. It was an ecstatic moment. Kalam was hoisted on the shoulders by his colleagues. In Trivandrum we were all welcomed as heroes when we stepped off the plane. My little sons were thrilled. In their school the SLV had been dubbed the Sea Loving Vehicle. And now their father's organization had been vindicated!

The successful SLV-3 flight was a real morale booster to ISRO. India had become the sixth member of the exclusive club of space-faring nations. Decades have passed by since then and this club has not increased in strength!

Two more successful flights followed and the credentials of SLV-3 were firmly established. The payload capability of SLV-3 was not significant. There was no future to it except to provide a learning platform for ISRO. And that it did in great measure indeed. A spectrum of technologies and concepts had been validated. A sound management system had been established, which could tap into all the available resources in the country.

The areas at ISRO where great strides were made during this time included high-energy solid propellant motors, fibreglass and Kevlar motor cases, precision fabrication including use of 15CDV6 steel cases, control thrusters using bipropellants, control components, avionics systems including inertial platforms, and a host of software used for establishing and operating a launch base. However, the most important factor was the confidence that the successes imparted – teams began work on building larger launch vehicles and more complex payloads. Significantly, out of the 1200 scientists and engineers who worked on the SLV-3 project, hardly a handful had had a foreign education. Our homegrown engineers were the ones who built our first satellite launch vehicle.

Many years later, during the silver jubilee celebrations of the first successful SLV flight, I heard many of the engineers who had been part of the core development team reminiscing about the early days when the facilities were basic. Some remembered using mechanical calculators, drafting boards with T-squares and computers which used punch cards. Even propellants were hand-mixed. As I listened to them, I felt proud that twenty-five years later, most of them were still there, working on advanced launch vehicles.

The fourth SLV-3 flight took off three years later on 30 August 1983. It was a roaring success. Prime Minister Indira Gandhi, who was our special guest that time, declared she was 'thrilled, excited and proud' to witness the launch from Sriharikota.

The successful launch of SLV-3 in 1980 followed by two more in the succeeding years had restored the confidence of the ISRO teams. Now we needed to increase the payload capacity of SLV-3 to at least 100 to 150 kg if we were to carry out any meaningful experiments in low earth orbit. The next task was therefore to augment the payload capacity of the vehicle. We decided that the simplest way to do this was to add strap-on motors to the first stage. In this way we could also try out a technique that could be used later for larger vehicles.

11

ASLV: Hurdling through to Success

After the successful second flight of SLV-3, Kalam had moved out of the project, which was taken over by Ved Prakash Sandlas. Around the same time, M.S.R. Dev, one of Kalam's 'boys', was appointed the project director of the Augmented Satellite Launch Vehicle (ASLV) project. The formal government sanction for this was received in 1982.

Kalam left ISRO the same year to join the Defence Research and Development Organization (DRDO) and take up the challenge of developing ballistic missiles for the defence services. His single-minded focus and ability to get things done were qualities which would help him inject some vibrancy into this crucial project which was languishing without firm direction. His assignment was a sort of indirect technology transfer between ISRO and DRDO in this vital field.

By 1984 four SLV-3 launches had taken place and ISRO was now ready to focus its full attention on the development of the ASLV. The SLV-3 programme was formally closed. This was also the year that Brahm Prakash passed away in Bombay.

M.S.R. Dev had said in his project report that the first launch of ASLV would take place in 1985, but a lot still had to be done. The hardware developed for SLV-3 formed the building blocks for ASLV. However, the aerodynamic simulation of the strap-ons was more complex and the jettisoning of the motors after burnout had to be smooth. For the first time a bulbous nose cone was used, to accommodate a larger spacecraft. It was also proposed to use a Closed Loop Guidance system (CLG) with an inertial platform, a digital autopilot and on-board computers. The Telemetry, Tracking and Command (TTC) system was also new and operated in the S-band. The launch base required a range of new facilities, including a new mobile launch tower and updated downrange tracking networks. Developing these systems and validating them for the flight was a mammoth task.

The launch date overshot the 1985 deadline specified in the project report. There were also major changes in the leadership at ISRO. In 1985, Satish Dhawan retired as chairman after thirteen years at the helm and U.R. Rao took over from him. Rao, until then, was not a launch vehicle insider. He had to gain a 'hands-on' feel for the issues facing launch vehicle development. He did this very fast, of course, as not only was he a very bright scientist, he was also an ISRO pioneer who had been associated with all the projects right from the very start.

Rao also had the unenviable task of dealing with senior engineers who were more or less his peers. He had to manage them tactfully if the project deadline was to be kept. There were some expected upheavals. Vasanth Gowariker, the pioneer propellant engineer, resigned from his post as director of VSSC and S.C. Gupta, the control, guidance and avionics specialist, took over from him. N. Pant, who was the director of SHAR, was moved to head ISAC in Bangalore and M.R. Kurup, a solid propellant specialist, took over from him. I became the associate director of VSSC.

It was 1987 by the time all the ASLV subsystems were ready, tested and validated, and moved to SHAR. The vehicle assembly started in the new vertical assembly facilities at the beginning of the year. ASLV and the associated ground systems including the downrange tracking systems were ready for the launch by March 1987.

I distinctly recall the upbeat atmosphere on the night before the launch day at the ASLV launch pad and in the associated blockhouse. The assembled rocket and umbilical tower glistened in the brightly lit pad. The launch complex itself, during the mission, resembled an Indian wedding locale with the sudden congregation of a large number of people of all sorts dashing about talking excitedly. The only difference was that their excitement was about highly technical issues!

The SHAR administration was stretched to its ultimate limits to provide logistics and ensure that the tempo of work did not suffer for want of facilities. Everyone was keyed up and working round the clock to ensure the success of the mission. U.R. Rao, the new ISRO chairman, went around the work centres cheering the engineers who had worked day and night to achieve this.

Prime Minister Rajiv Gandhi was coming to watch the launch. So were N.T. Rama Rao, the chief minister of Andhra Pradesh, and Andhra Pradesh Governor Kumudben Joshi. The next day all operational personnel were at their workplaces. NTR, dressed in his dramatic saffron robes, came with a large contingent of officials. Rajiv Gandhi was his usual affable self, speaking words of encouragement to all the scientists.

The countdown proceeded. The key people were back at their consoles in the control centre. Final clearances were given for the launch. At around noon on 24 March 1987 the final countdown was completed, and at zero, the vehicle zoomed dramatically into space.

The senior personnel, as usual, were intently glued to their consoles, but others, including the VIPs, were out on the terrace watching the take-off. Thousands of others watched with bated breath from viewing galleries and the terraces in the colonies. The rise of the vehicle was pretty impressive and the strap-on motors fired perfectly. The crowd outside cheered and clapped wildly, but tension inside the control room was palpable, for we knew that we had a long way to go!

Less than a minute into the flight we knew something had gone wrong. After the burn of the strap-on motors the first stage was supposed to ignite, but we did not see the telltale bright plume that would indicate that all was well. Obviously the stage had not ignited for some reason and the lifeless rocket started losing height.

The tracking teams soon announced the loss of signals from the satellite. The second stage and the heat shield separated from the vehicle. From total elation we plunged into dismay as we saw our beloved rocket taking a sharp U-turn and go hurtling into the Bay of Bengal. What could have gone wrong? It was a real blow to the organization, particularly to VSSC.

The response of the nation and the media was quite positive and encouraging. Gupta, the VSSC director, urged his dejected colleagues to mount full efforts to identify the problem and to correct the defects so as to realize the next launch within twelve months. At a gathering of employees after the launch, we tried to come to terms with our loss. NTR addressed the gathering and got so carried away with his own rhetoric that he almost went into a tailspin, like the rocket we had just launched!

'Please sit, swamiji,' Rajiv Gandhi was heard urging the Andhra CM.

Rajiv Gandhi addressed the scientists and praised their hard work. 'Don't lose heart,' he said. 'It is only a setback in time. It is only when you stumble that you can get up and walk better.'

U.R. Rao immediately appointed a Failure Analysis Committee (FAC) under my chairmanship to analyse the available data, identify possible reasons for the failure of the mission, and suggest remedial measures to be incorporated in the subsequent flights. This was later on named the Aravamudan Committee. We were to review the entire sequence of operation from countdown to the termination of the flight, and look for any clues from the telemetry, tracking and visual data that would lead us to the cause of the failure.

We had seven sittings. We met at Trivandrum, Sriharikota and Bangalore, and received inputs from several expert committees. We consulted experienced specialists like Kalam, Sandlas and others associated with SLV-3. We listened patiently to any individual from the working teams with any ideas. We carefully examined the masses of data gathered from the telemetry recordings, tracking data, photographs, video recordings and also the pre-flight checkout parameters. We studied in great detail the design calculations, getting inputs from the quality teams. We inspected the debris collected at the launch base. And wherever possible, we carried out computer simulations.

Soon it became quite clear that the cause of mission failure was the non-ignition of the first stage at T+48.7 seconds. The environmental factors recorded during the flight seemed to be within acceptable limits. The committee now eliminated all other causes of failure except those relating to the actual passage of firing current through the igniter. This, we felt, could have been caused by a possible short circuit in the redundant ignition circuits, or an open circuit. A random malfunction of the electromechanical safe/arm device was also not ruled out.

After the painstaking analysis by the committee, these conclusions were a bit open-ended, since it was not possible to unequivocally pinpoint the cause of failure. However, we made a series of recommendations for the next flight, including modifications in the firing circuits, elimination of the electromechanical safe/arm device and improvements in several other systems. We also suggested that careful ground qualification tests should be carried out wherever possible. What was more worrying was the fact that only a fraction of the entire ASLV mission had had an opportunity to be flight-tested. Now there was always the background fear as to what other failures were lurking in the remaining systems.

The organization took more than a year to implement all the suggestions we made. Extra care was taken while assembling and testing all the subsystems, particularly the ignition systems. We wanted to ensure that a similar failure never occurred again. And, sure enough that failure mode was not repeated. But worse was in store!

The second ASLV flight finally took off on the afternoon of 13 July 1988. This time, too, the strap-on rockets fired beautifully and the vehicle rose majestically into the sky. People waited breathlessly for the sign of ignition of the first stage. There was a big round of applause when it fired, but we were worried. It seemed a bit behind time.

Around fifty seconds after take-off we noticed some instability in the vehicle, which seemed out of control. This was exactly the time when the control had to switch over from the strap-on burning phase to the core stage burning. The loss of control had a disastrous effect and resulted in large structural loads on the vehicle. It broke up spectacularly in midair, leaving us devastated.

The failure mode was different, but it had occurred around the same time as the first flight. Fundamental doubts began to appear in the minds of the specialists. Was the basic design of the vehicle faulty? A large amount of public money was involved and answers needed to be given. The nation had been very understanding when the first mission failed, but this time the public was not so forgiving. The morale of the teams was at its lowest ebb. Thousands of man-hours of work had gone into the programme, and there was a feeling of dejection and frustration among the scientific community.

U.R. Rao immediately constituted an internal FAC, headed by the VSSC director S.C. Gupta, as well as a national level Expert Review Panel (ERP), with the eminent aeronautical scientist Roddam Narasimha as chairman. The members were drawn from all over the country. I was on this committee as well. The two committees worked hard for more than a year with unprecedented thoroughness and objectivity. The results of the painstaking analyses of the internal committee were fed to the ERP. Anyone with any opinion on the failure mode or design issues was patiently heard, including sometimes mavericks with strange ideas.

For example, there was this young professor of aerospace engineering from a university in north India who had a string of impressive degrees. He started addressing press conferences saying he had determined after scientific calculations that there was a gravitational anomaly over Sriharikota which meant it would be impossible to orbit satellites from there. He did not approach the ISRO specialists but talked to various newspapers, insisting that ISRO was wasting precious resources and should move the launch pad to some more suitable location. With the unfortunate failure of two successive ASLV flights the professor assumed an 'I told you so' attitude and his voice became louder, although the failure mechanisms of the two flights had absolutely nothing to do with his claims.

After the second unsuccessful flight, the chairman of the FAC, who was himself a very eminent aerospace scientist, decided to leave no stone unturned and invited the professor to address us. Although he himself did not give credence to the professor's theory, he decided to give the man a chance to share his 'scientific calculations' with us.

We paid the professor's airfare. He arrived at VSSC where we had organized a full-fledged discussion with the senior specialists of the committee. Soon it became very apparent that he had nothing worthwhile to say. Finally, the professor admitted that there was an error in his calculations and he left to catch his flight back from the Trivandrum airport. Lo and behold, the next day we read in the papers that he had addressed the press at the airport and told them he had educated the FAC about their mistaken calculations! We never heard from him again after the subsequent successful ASLV and PSLV launchings. What would he have to say now after our spectacularly successful moon and Mars missions, I wonder!

The failure of the second launch was attributed to the quick build-up of yaw errors about fifty seconds into the flight, which resulted in forces on the vehicle much above the design limits. This led to its break-up. The vehicle was found to be inherently unstable in the yaw plane. This normally would have been taken care of, if the control were effective. It was determined that a combination of low autopilot gain, particularly during the transition from strap-on to the core stage burning, and adverse atmospheric conditions had contributed to the loss of control.

The recommendations and remedial measures suggested by the FAC and ERP were quite comprehensive. These covered many areas: specification, engineering, simulation, testing, quality control, reliability and so on. Modifications were suggested in the autopilot design. It was also felt that it was essential to use a 'real-time decision-making' system for determining the correct time for the core ignition. We also needed more realistic prediction of the action times of the motors and improved modelling of the Secondary Injection Thrust Vector Control (SITVC) system. The committee also suggested the possible use of fins and many other modifications.

The ERP had a word of encouragement to the teams. It expressed confidence in the teams' ability and skill in solving all technological issues, if necessary using inputs from other agencies in the country. It also noted that most developed countries had passed through similar phases in their early development efforts. The teams set to work on the corrective measures in earnest and took more than two years to come out with a modified vehicle.

By the time the ASLV vehicle was assembled on the launch tower for the third time in 1992, more changes in management had occurred. Kurup had retired and I was in charge of SHAR. The payload was a Stretched Rohini Scientific Satellite (SROSS-C, for short) weighing 105 kg.

ASLV-D3 was launched on 20 May 1992, almost three years after I took over. This mission was a perfect success.

The SROSS-C spacecraft went smoothly into a low earth orbit. The ISRO teams heaved a collective sigh of relief. Two years later, on 4 May 1994, we had one more successful launch of the ASLV-D4 carrying the SROSS-C2 satellite.

There were many who questioned the need for developing ASLV, which by itself had no application. But in my opinion ASLV provided ISRO with invaluable experience in rocket technology. This kind of information is normally not available in the public domain because of its strategic nature. It provided a low-cost precursor to the more important and expensive polar satellite launch vehicle PSLV, which became the workhorse of ISRO, capable of launching remote sensing satellites of more than 1 tonne class into polar orbits. Many common technology elements were validated. The strap-on technology, inertial navigation, closed loop guidance systems, digital autopilot, real-time decision-making, bulbous heat shields, S-band TTC, vertical integration and so on, all tried out and perfected in the ASLV, could be used in the PSLV. Also, most importantly, the teams learned that rocketry is unforgiving and called for a totally disciplined approach to ensure quality and reliability.

12

Sultan of SHAR

Meanwhile, there were many changes in my personal life. When I became director of SHAR in October 1989 I had to uproot myself from Trivandrum where I had spent over twenty-five years of my working life. We had to rent out the house we had built in Ulloor in a small colony called Saptharang, created by some of us from ISRO. Seven languages were spoken in our little colony of a dozen houses, and over the years we had become like one big joint family.

Gita moved to SHAR a few months after I did, when our older son Ananth left for Bangalore to join an engineering college. Our younger son Sriram came with us to join the SHAR Central School. SHAR was a total contrast to Trivandrum. It was home to a rather insular space community that lived in peaceful isolation far from the madding crowd. Surrounded by Pulicat Lake, the Bay of Bengal and Buckingham Canal, Sriharikota was an island with a 50 km coastline and an area of about 44,000 acres. There were thousands of employees, temporary and permanent, living in the housing colonies.

And I was the Big Boss. My friends and colleagues dubbed me the 'Sultan of SHAR', although I must confess I sometimes felt more like the Count of Monte Cristo imprisoned on an island.

In the early days all the housing was within the island, but as the numbers increased we had spilled over into the tiny adjoining town of Sullurupeta. We now had a total population exceeding 10,000 and all the civic amenities had to be provided by ISRO. So we had a large Central School, a hospital, basic shopping, transportation, a police outpost, a temple, a church, a mosque, burial and cremation grounds, and, of course, a large security establishment in the form of a CISF contingent. As the director, I often felt more like a municipal chairman!

Life was pretty hectic during the launch campaigns. Operating the range facilities was our main task. But we also had to take care of a floating population of scientists, engineers, technicians, administrative personnel, logistics providers and others who would descend on us for a launch. They were a tense, on-the-edge crowd who had to be provided with food and a place to crash. Doctors had to be on call to see they didn't break down or burn out.

And then there were the VIP visitors who had to be entertained. They needed special security and their staff had to be accommodated as well. Amidst all the chaos, the technical tasks and the countdown had to proceed with utmost precision. Whenever possible we would try to persuade VIPs with special security to come and leave a day or two before the launch so that we could focus on the work at hand. But, if a VVIP like the prime minister of India decided to 'grace' the occasion, the range would be virtually taken over by the police and secret service. At such times, even legitimate technical personnel manning the campaign were sometimes prevented from moving about freely.

At one launch campaign, I was on my way to escort our VVIP guest, Prime Minister P.V. Narasimha Rao, to the launch pad when my car was blocked by the special security. They just would not let me proceed even though I explained to them that I was the director of the centre and had to reach the launch pad before the PM. Finally, a senior police officer took pity on me, put me in his car and rushed me to the launch pad in time to receive Narasimha Rao.

A sad and strange period was when Rajiv Gandhi was assassinated. He had witnessed a launch a couple of years before and had offered words of encouragement to the scientists who were feeling desolate after the failure of the launch. It was difficult to come to terms with his loss, as he had always been very proactive as far as ISRO was concerned.

I remember how I heard the shocking news. It was past midnight on 21 May 1991 and I was fast asleep when the telephone rang persistently. I woke up with a start. Usually SHAR was quite peaceful when there was no campaign and I could not imagine who would ring me in the middle of the night. Since it was a hot summer night, my first thought was that a fire had broken out in the forest.

It was the CISF commandant at the other end. 'Sir, something terrible has happened,' he said. 'We just received intelligence that the former prime minister Rajiv Gandhi has been assassinated by a suicide bomber while addressing a rally in Sriperumbedur, near Chennai.'

There was chaos and anger all around. We had a large CISF contingent and I asked the commandant to put his men on alert and to be in touch with the police authorities in case of any emergencies.

I remembered the day when Indira Gandhi was assassinated back in 1984. There was much mob violence in Trivandrum where I was stationed at that time. We could not run our buses and all of us had to walk back from Thumba which was 20 km away. Even our children had to walk home from school. I knew it was unlikely that violence of that nature would erupt on the island of Sriharikota, but I had to also make sure that our employees living in Sullurpeta were safe and that they could travel to work without incident. Those were tension-filled days. Soon, the police identified the assassin as an LTTE member and many arrests followed. The mastermind Sivarasan had fled the scene and was reported to be somewhere in the vicinity. There were all kinds of rumours as to where he was hiding. Many people claimed to have spotted him.

Things seemed to be settling down when suddenly one morning I woke up and found two armed security guards standing outside my house. I called the CISF commandant to find out the reason. He said he could not discuss it over the phone and drove down to my residence to tell me. Apparently he had had secret word from the Intelligence Bureau that Sivarasan, who was still on the run, had taken the sea route from Chennai and was trying to land somewhere on the Sriharikota coast. We had a vast coastline and there were many casuarina groves where he could hide. He could even be hiding in the reserve forest area.

The commandant told me that Sivarasan might have plans to take a senior central government official hostage and use him to bargain with the government for his own escape. Since I was the director of the centre and the most senior official in Sriharikota, he had strict instruction to provide me with round-the-clock armed security.

And so I got pushed into this security cordon, which I found most unnerving. We had guards outside our house much to the annoyance of my school-going son Sriram who said his friends now refused to visit him! My personal guard travelled with me from my home to my office, which was less than half a kilometre away. He squeezed into the front seat of my car when I had to travel to Madras en route to other places. Even when I went for an evening walk the security man used to follow me ten steps behind. This protocol continued for quite some time until Sivarasan was cornered and shot somewhere in Bangalore.

Life in SHAR was very different from life in Trivandrum. In Trivandrum we had lived very close to nature, surrounded as we were by coconut groves and paddy fields and beaches. In SHAR we lived even closer to nature, but it was of a different kind. The forest was all around us. At night we could hear jackals howling outside our compound and the snorts of wild boars.

One of the strange sights in SHAR was that of the 'wild' cows walking nonchalantly past the security gates to graze in the forest. All these cows had owners who lived in the colonies and every evening after they finished their grazing they would return home to be milked. The fresh and delicious milk was preferred by most people to the packet milk brought in from outside the island.

SHAR was also full of birds. Migratory birds from as far away as Russia would fly here to escape the harsh winter in their home. The Bombay Natural History Society had set up a small unit in SHAR to study birdlife, and we would often go to watch them ringing the birds. During the winter season Pulicat Lake became a bird-watchers' paradise. We just had to walk out of the main gate and on to the paved road that now connected our island to the mainland to feast our eyes on a variety of exotic waterbirds. Huge flocks of flamingoes turned the horizon pink. Close to the shore there would be painted storks, pelicans, varieties of ducks, egrets and many other migratory birds. Employees coming from Sullurpeta would stop on their way to work to enjoy the sight.

Our chief photographer in SHAR, Seetharaman, apart from taking great pictures of our launches, also took many beautiful pictures of the birds and of nature in Sriharikota. Satish Dhawan wrote a small book on the aerodynamics of bird flight and used some of Seetharaman's pictures and film strips to illustrate it.

Nature sometimes intruded into our technical spaces as well. Such as feral bees. They were huge and vicious, and they had built large hives on the upper stages of our tall Mobile Service Tower (MST). Naturally our employees were afraid to go anywhere near them. I tried several measures to get rid of the hives, but they somehow always managed to come back.

The Yenadi the original inhabitants of SHAR, still lived inside the forest in their own special, conical cyclone-proof huts. Over the years many of them had got educated and quite a few were employed by us. Cycling was the most popular form of transport on the island and we would find everyone, ranging from top officers and their wives and children to the Yenadi cycling along the beautiful, straight tree-lined roads.

At SHAR, the employees were quite busy, immersed in their campaigns and day-to-day work. Women employees with school-going children actually preferred working in this centre because life was simple and safe. Everything including the school was within cycling distance and in an emergency they could get home within minutes. But for the homebound wives, SHAR could often be quite suffocating. Some of the wives were themselves well qualified but had no opportunity to use their education. This sometimes led to depression, especially when the children finished their schooling and flew the nest. Gita started the Sriharikota Women's Association (SWAS) in an attempt to give them a social and cultural outlet.

Many major facilities which needed my attention were coming up fast. Our little island was growing into a major spaceport and I was confident that in the not-too-distant future we would be launching world-class spacecraft.

13

Growing Pains

The late 1980s and early '90s were times of both hope and despair. This was the tumultuous period when we were poised on the threshold of a major expansion. We had had some successful SLV flights but the first and second experimental flights of ASLV had met with disastrous failures in 1987 and 1988. It took four more years for ISRO to recover from those setbacks. We had to systematically learn from the large amount of data accumulated before we could achieve another successful launch.

In 1989, when I arrived in SHAR, preparations were on for the next ASLV flight. Side by side we were building up launch facilities for the much larger PSLV flight. SHAR was also busy with the casting and static testing of the huge solid propellant motor of the PSLV. We were on the verge of completing a major engineering feat: the giant Mobile Service Tower (MST), weighing more than 3000 tonnes, was almost ready for handling the PSLV launchings. But before that could happen, we had to pass a couple of more milestones.

ISRO was expanding very rapidly. Major facilities were coming up in different locations to cater to the systems required for the development of various new elements of PSLV. Already, by the mid-1980s, a centre for assembling and testing the liquid propulsion systems had been established in Mahendragiri near Nagarcoil in Tamil Nadu. This barren, sparsely populated forest area in the foothills of the Western Ghats was chosen after a countrywide search for a location where the hazardous chemicals used in ground testing of rockets containing liquid fuels would not harm the ground water even if they ultimately found their way into the soil. The huge flame deflectors under the towering static test stands on which the large rocket engines were fired, were built into the hills, taking advantage of the natural formation.

The Mahendragiri project was initially stalled following press reports that claimed there were populations of endangered lion-tailed macaque living in these forests. Subsequent studies revealed there was hardly any animal life in the forest area, which wasn't really virgin forest as it was made out to be. Ultimately we hoped to also test our mammoth cryogenic engines at Mahendragiri.

A Liquid Propulsion Systems Centre (LPSC) was set up in Valiamala, a scenic area close to Trivandrum. This is where the precision components for liquid-fuelled rockets are now developed. The integration of the equipment bay and components and subsystems for the liquid engines is also done here. LPSC focuses on crucial parts which require precision engineering. For example, the thrust vector control and reaction control systems used both in the spacecraft and launch vehicles are assembled here. These tiny rockets actually provide the muscle power to place a satellite into its precise orbit or to nudge a gigantic launch vehicle into the right trajectory. Similarly, the Apogee Kick Motor (AKM), a small rocket used to correct the satellite's initial orbit after launch, is also assembled here. The AKM is fired at a precise intermediate point to kick the spacecraft from an elliptical into a more desirable near-circular orbit.

Other liquid motors developed at LPSC are used to correct the attitude of the satellite and position it so that it looks in the right direction. They are indispensable for such precision manoeuvres because, unlike their solid fuel counterparts, they can be shut off and started at any time. And they are more fuel-efficient. Similar control rockets are used even in the launch vehicles to control orientation.

Other installations which came up in this period included a unit for manufacturing carbon and fibreglass products at Vattiyoorkavu, a suburb of Trivandrum, and a factory at Alwaye for producing ammonium perchlorate, an essential ingredient for the solid propellants.

Amidst this frenetic increase in the tempo of activities, we at SHAR were focusing on ensuring a successful ASLV launch to be followed by the larger PSLV. The third ASLV flight in May 1992 was my first important mission as the director of SHAR. I was filled with a great feeling of relief and triumph when it turned out to be a grand success. There was a palpable lifting of the depression and distress which the ISRO community had felt after the two failed ASLV missions. The flight also validated many technologies which were to be employed in future missions like PSLV.

But there was no time for us to rest on our laurels. The preparations for the first experimental launch of PSLV were already afoot. By mid-1993 the vehicle was getting assembled on the new MST. When this was going on, I had sleepless nights worrying about the safety of the vehicle on the pad, loaded with enormous quantities of solid and liquid propellants. The monsoon months are a real nightmare at SHAR which is a notoriously cyclone-prone region. The rains and cyclonic winds could wreak havoc – especially since we were handling hazardous material.

This was our first experimental PSLV launch. It would carry the 846 kg IRS-1E which was derived from an engineering model of IRS-1A. This satellite had an optical payload and a German instrument called the Monocular Electro-optical Stereo Scanner.

The suspense and excitement in the team was palpable as D-Day approached. The launch was set for 20 September 1993, with the take-off scheduled for 10.42 am. The countdown had commenced seventy-two hours prior to that. The loading of the liquid propellants had gone on all night before the launch.

The launch campaign involved coordinating the preparedness of a variety of teams including those on the launch pad and in the control centre. They had to be in sync with the safety crew and the tracking groups in the range and in the downrange stations. The spacecraft specialists had to work in tandem with all of them. VIPs and other visitors, local government and police officials had to be taken care of. Meanwhile, the routine work of the centre and the township had to proceed normally as well.

The countdown progressed without any breaks and the 3000 tonne MST was moved back to its prelaunch parking position. A final station check was called and the mission director G. Madhavan Nair authorized the launch.

I was at my console in the front row of the control room. I sat next to the ISRO Chairman U.R. Rao's console. Gupta, Kasturirangan, Pant and Madhavan Nair sat in the same row. There was dead silence in the control room as we reached the final ten seconds of counting. We heaved a huge sigh of relief as we saw the roll control thrusters lighting at T-2 seconds.

As we reached count 'zero', we could see the first stage igniting and the huge 300 tonne monster rising majestically from the launch tower. The thunderous roar reached us a few seconds later. There was the usual jubilation and hand clapping by the visitors in the room, but we in the front row knew that the action had just begun and we had a long way to go.

Rao was on the intercom urging people to stop clapping and wait for all the mission events to finish. The jubilation was understandable since all the initial events which were visible seemed to have taken place at the right time, particularly during the most difficult part of the trajectory when the vehicle was expected to experience severe atmospheric loads.

The strap-ons, the first stage and the second stage seemed to have functioned as predicted. The separation after burnout was perfect. The heat shield protecting the satellite in the dense atmospheric region also separated correctly at the right altitude above 100 km. When the third stage was ignited it fired with the correct thrust and also burned for the right amount of time.

And then it happened! The entire vehicle suddenly went into a dramatic uncontrolled angular rotation. Obviously the rocket had fallen short of its altitude because of a reduced velocity.

We sat transfixed staring at our monitor screens, too dazed to even think. All we knew at that moment was that the maiden flight of PSLV, on which we had pinned so much hope, could not achieve enough velocity to inject IRS-1E into earth orbit.

Before take-off, Madhavan Nair, the project director, was full of confidence that the mission would be successful, given the extensive prelaunch testing and validation that had taken place. Now he was totally devastated. I saw him weeping with disappointment. But I couldn't go and console him because U.R. Rao had slumped into a chair in the control room, speechless. I was worried about him.

Rao wanted to immediately summon all the specialists with the available telemetry information. He was anxious to see what had gone wrong. But I knew that everyone was washed out with fatigue. We had been up all night during the countdown, and were hardly in a situation to think rationally about what could have gone wrong. I had a difficult time convincing him to rest and allow the team to calmly go through the data. I escorted him, along with his wife who had come to witness the launching, to their room in the guest house to get some sleep before resuming any further analysis of the failure.

Meanwhile, the control centre was buzzing with conjecture. Obviously, the separation of the second stage had imparted an unexpectedly large disturbance. This in turn must have rendered the flexible nozzle control system of the third stage quite inadequate. So, the satellite had gone into a suborbital flight.

The mission was officially declared a failure, although most of the technology elements had actually worked well. We were by now quite nervous. An estimate at that time put the incremental cost of each PSLV vehicle at about Rs 50 crores, not counting the cost of infrastructure created to build it. The total budgeted cost for the PSLV project was of the order of Rs 415 crores. This was a large sum of money and we could not afford to have too many failures.

This time N. Pant, who was the vice chairman of ISRO, was put in charge of the FAC. Fortunately a wealth of information in the form of telemetry and tracking data was available. Teams were formed to carry out extensive simulation and ground tests. And the failure mode, which was soon identified, turned out to be quite simple and straightforward.

There was an arithmetical error in the software of the on-board computer in calculating the error voltage which needed to be applied to the gimbal system to bring the vehicle under control. Unfortunately the extensive ground testing could not uncover this error, since the amplitude of the simulated errors never reached the flight values. The committee also found that two retro rockets failed to fire during the second stage separation; this seemed to have caused a collision between the spent second stage and the third stage, leading to a large disturbance prior to the third stage firing.

These were such trivial errors. How we wished these could have been avoided! The maiden PSLV launch would then have been a spectacular success. But, in retrospect, I think it was important that such hidden and potential failure modes came to light at the earliest so that future missions could be successful. The organization learned very valuable early lessons which helped the PSLV rocket become one of ISRO's most reliable workhorses.

It took more than a year for ISRO to recover from the failure of this first launch. During the year we worked hard to address all possible areas of potential failure modes. In the midst of all this, in April 1994, I moved to Bangalore to take charge as the director of the ISRO Satellite Centre (ISAC). U.R. Rao had retired and when Kasturirangan, the ISAC director, became the new ISRO chairman, I replaced him at ISAC. However, I continued to hold charge as director of SHAR for a few more months, as we wanted to ensure continuity until the next ASLV launch scheduled in May 1994.

Kasturirangan turned out to be a lucky mascot for ISRO – his first rocket mission as ISRO chairman was a thumping success. Sreenivasan, who took over from me as director of SHAR, was at the helm for the second launch of PSLV which took off on 15 October 1994. The countdown was smooth and so was the lift-off of the vehicle. Within seventeen minutes after the launch, the IRS-P2 satellite it carried was injected into a sun synchronous orbit – a requirement for most remote sensing missions. There was great jubilation all around.

Madhavan Nair, the PSLV project director, was the man of the hour and was mobbed by his colleagues and congratulated. More than 3000 engineers in ISRO and a large number from other partner industries and academic institutions had worked very hard for this day. The launch was an example of perfect coordination between a variety of agencies in India and abroad focusing on a single objective. The media and the politicians were lavish in their praise. Kasturirangan called it a 'textbook launch' – a phrase he was to use often in the years to come.

The PSLV workhorse became the stud of our stable. Not only that, our own homegrown PSLV became one of the most reliable rockets in its category in the world, earning global admiration. Nations vied with one another to get their remote sensing satellites launched by it. And ISRO never looked back.

14

The Story of GSLV

By the early 1990s, while I was working on augmenting the facilities at our spaceport, my colleagues at VSSC were working on the next ambitious rocket we would launch from there: the Geosynchronous Launch Vehicle (GSLV). And therein lies another tale. The story of GSLV revolves around the development of a cryogenic upper stage. But let me go back a little so we can have an idea of how and why the events unfolded as they did and why we had to struggle so hard to get our cryogenic engine.

In a 1970 paper read at a national electronics conference, Sarabhai had talked about a national geosynchronous satellite for television and telecommunication to be launched for India by western countries. He had coined the term INSAT and listed the many applications of such a satellite which would dramatically advance India's development. At the end of the paper he had also said, rather hesitantly, that within a ten-year time frame we should aim not just to build such satellites in India but also to build Indian launch vehicles capable of launching them into geosynchronous orbits from our launch pad at Sriharikota.

A year after he presented his paper, Sarabhai was gone. We knew we had to fulfil his dream, but obviously we had a long, long way to go. We had not even started on the SLV programme then. Dhawan gave the launch vehicle development a kick-start, but since we needed to get our basics right, he wanted us to concentrate initially on SLV and ASLV. Both these vehicles used solid rocket stages. By themselves they were nothing more than technology demonstration devices as a prelude to building much larger vehicles to orbit heavier payloads.

Side by side, however, we were also planning and designing PSLV. We knew we would need engines that used liquid propellant for this. Just as we were looking around for the right technology, an exciting new possibility opened up. In the early 1970s we got a very tempting offer to collaborate with a French firm named SEP which was making rocket engines using earth storable liquid propellants.

France needed 10,000 aerospace quality pressure transducers for their Ariane launch vehicle. Obviously it would be cheaper to produce these in India and the French who had collaborated with us on many programmes knew we had the capability of setting up a specialized production unit. What they offered in return was hugely exciting. They said they would transfer the technology of their Viking engine, which used liquid propellant.

Dhawan set the teams into action. The contract was signed under the able guidance of T.N. Seshan who was then in charge of the negotiations. The redoubtable Seshan, who later on became the chief election commissioner of India, made sure we got the best deal possible. Under this agreement our engineers got to work alongside the French engineers on the highly specialized Viking engine, which the French were just developing then. Nambi Narayanan led the team of ISRO engineers deputed to work at the facility in France.

It might be interesting here to note that the French Viking engine used to power their Ariane ran into quite a few problems, while Vikas, the engine we developed in India based on this technology, became the mainstay of our PSLV. But that is another story.

Even in those early days we knew that the GSLV we planned to launch in the future was of a different class. It would need an upper stage using more efficient propellants to take the much heavier payloads to geosynchronous altitudes (about 36,000 km). And the only answer was cryogenic propellants, namely liquid oxygen and liquid hydrogen.

Liquid oxygen and hydrogen are extremely hazardous substances needing very careful handling and storage facilities. Even advanced countries had taken decades to master this technology. In the early 1970s, there were quite a few specialists who felt that ISRO should immediately start the development of cryogenic engines because they knew that without these engines it was impossible to attain a geosynchronous capability. Dhawan was fully aware of this but was hesitant to commit ISRO to a complex developmental task when the organization was struggling with the much simpler SLV and ASLV development. By the time he retired, ISRO had barely recovered from the initial failure of the first SLV-3 flight and had just staggered back to its feet. By the end of his tenure, we had just managed to launch three more successful SLV-3 flights.

The irony is that we could have actually got our cryogenic engine in the early 1970s itself, but we missed the chance. When the Vikas engine programme was started, SEP was in some kind of crisis. They had offered to sign a similar collaborative deal with ISRO for a cryogenic engine which they were in the process of developing. But ISRO regrettably did not consider this seriously. If only we had grabbed that opportunity, we could have perhaps gained decades in the acquisition of cryo technology. Anyway there was nothing much we could do now about this lost opportunity.

ISRO started looking around for an agency that would supply us not only cryo engines but also the technology. Very soon we started getting offers from established companies with expertise in this area. The first offer came in 1988 from General Dynamics, the American company that had designed and built the Atlas Centaur launch vehicle in the 1980s. They wanted to sell us two cryogenic engines which they felt could be adapted and used in our launch vehicle. They would also transfer the technology to us at a cost.

But their charges were unaffordable. The two engines alone would have cost us about US$ 800 million. And what if the US government suddenly decided they would not permit the technology transfer? Then ISRO would have to keep buying expensive rockets from General Motors to sustain the programme. Arianespace also made a similar offer in 1989, but the cost was even higher.

Since nothing was working out, we were gearing up to develop our own cryo engine, when the Russians came into the picture. The Russian firm Glavkosmos offered to sell us two operational 12 tonne cryogenic engines and also transfer technology at a fraction of the cost of the US offer. This would enable us to build our own flight-worthy engine for the third launch. They also promised to transfer documents and drawings, and sell us all the material we might need to build the engines. ISRO decided to go in for this exciting deal. Eight years had been budgeted for developing our own technology from scratch, but this deal could help us to leapfrog ahead. There was now hope that our own engines would be ready within four years.

The contract with Glavkosmos was signed in 1991. A whole team of engineers got ready to go to Russia for training. R. Jeyamani, a senior mechanical engineer, experienced in rocket engines and propulsion, was working with me at Sriharikota when he was named project director for GSLV. Nambi Narayanan, another senior mechanical engineer, was put in charge of the cryo team. Other specialists were assigned to go to Russia and study various aspects of the fabrication technology.

We were more than a year into the project when the blow fell. The US suddenly announced that our agreement with the USSR violated the Missile Technology Control Regime (MTCR). There had been some rumblings, of course, and we had anticipated trouble – but not trouble of this magnitude.

The MTCR was supposed to be a watchdog body mandated to prevent nuclear proliferation. The signatories wanted to prevent missile technology from falling into irresponsible hands. However, over the years it had acquired a kind of Big Brother attitude. The signatories, led by the US, started imposing embargos even on small components that had even the remotest possibility of being used for making missiles.

ISRO had already been facing this situation for a while. Actually, we needed very few of the banned components. Developing them indigenously, therefore, was often impractical because it was time consuming and expensive. Still, knowing the situation could worsen at any point of time, we had already started developing many components on our own. We had also identified some alternative sources from where we could acquire essential components. This forethought stood us in great stead when the axe finally fell.

When cryogenic engines were declared as part of banned technology because they could be used in missiles, we found it laughable at first. Why would we want to use those dangerous-to-handle, cumbersome cryo engines which needed special launch pads when our own indigenously developed solid propellant rockets and boosters like PSLV were of much more practical use in missile technology? Had the fact that our PSLV been tested and proven sent jitters up their collective spine? Was banning the transfer of cryo technology just a knee-jerk reaction? After all our PSLV had the third largest solid booster in the world and was next only to the boosters powering the Space Shuttle and the Titan. Maybe that was what was bothering the US.

The Americans always knew about the negotiations between India and the USSR, which were done quite openly. It was shocking that they had chosen to suddenly create a problem much after the contract was signed and after half the contract value had been paid.

The then Indian prime minister, P.V. Narasimha Rao, as well as Russian President Gorbachev protested, but to no avail. The US imposed a two-year ban on the export or import of various components and also prohibited the signing of any new contracts with ISRO and Glavkosmos during this period. This ban also had a retrospective element to it, which meant that even contracts signed and paid for before the ban was imposed now stood rescinded.

The implications of this were quite monumental. It meant that our INSAT projects would be affected and this in turn would hit our satellite communication networks, which were totally dependent on our own satellites. Fortunately we had already started developing our own components and we were also sourcing some of them from other friendly countries. But there would still be a major setback because of the ban.

U.R. Rao, who as the chairman of ISRO, was the architect of the ISRO–Glavkosmos deal, tried his best to salvage the situation. He managed to get the Americans agree to review the retrospective clause of the ban on a case-to-case basis. But, despite his best efforts, the agreement with Glavkosmos continued on its downward spiral because of the political turmoil in the USSR. Gorbachev's successor Boris Yelstin crumbled under US pressure. Many discussions later the Russians and Indians reached some sort of middle ground.

Glavkosmos would sell some fully qualified cryo engines as well as some mock-ups but would not transfer any technology. Meanwhile, at ISRO we decided to revive our own indigenous cryo-engine programme in a more active fashion.

ISRO's troubles did not end there. Nambi Narayanan, the senior scientist in charge of the GSLV project, got falsely implicated in the infamous ISRO spy scandal. Nambi had joined us in the late 1960s. I still vividly remember my first meeting with him at Indra Bhavan in Trivandrum. He was about twenty-three years old and I could tell straight away that he was exceptionally bright. He had a mechanical engineering degree and was already working in a factory somewhere down south. He had heard of Thumba and thought it might offer interesting possibilities, but he wanted to be sure before he gave up his job. The landlord of the lodge where I lived in Trivandrum brought him to me and I spoke to him about TERLS and its exciting proposed activities. I told him we were focusing on scientific work using sounding rockets and that we ultimately hoped to build our sounding rockets ourselves. Obviously it all sounded exciting to him because he decided to join us. Thinking back, it seems almost unbelievable that within a couple of decades Nambi had successfully worked on rockets of magnitudes and complexities much beyond what we had envisioned during our brief conversation that day in Trivandrum.

Nambi proved to be a very smart and clever engineer. At first he worked under Kalam who was heading the rocket engineering division at TERLS. Then he was placed under Muthunayagam to work on rocket propulsion and was incorporated into a programme for building solid rocket motors. He was even sent to Princeton where he acquired an MS degree.

Since Nambi had worked with SEP during the Vikas engine project he had proven ability to handle technology transfer. That is why he was asked to head a similar mission to Russia for the cryo technology transfer. He was well entrenched in the project when the spy scandal broke out. The accusation against him was that he was trying to pass on secret documents relating to cryo technology to some spies from the Maldives. Poor Nambi even spent time in prison. Ultimately he was cleared but by then the damage had been done to his career.

The only redeeming feature in all this mess was that although ISRO got a severe jolt with all the adverse media coverage and Nambi himself was put through extreme distress, the issue did not seriously impact our work. The turmoil caused by the break-up of the Soviet Union impacted our cryogenic engine programme more than this scandal.

The Americans tried all possible ways to disrupt the programme. We faced embargoes all the time. The Russians were also frequently pressurized to change contractual clauses and cost elements or cancel parts of the contract. So we were constantly on our toes, looking out for alternate strategies and trying to find new sources. Obviously all this caused considerable delays and derailed the schedules of many activities.

Cryogenic engine development was already a very difficult field and there was hardly any information available in the public domain. This meant we had to struggle with considerable trial and error during our developmental process.

Meanwhile, the Russians were building the cryogenic engine and stage for our programme as per our salvaged contract. SHAR was gearing up the facilities required in the launch base for handling, storing and loading the liquid hydrogen and oxygen propellants. Things got really complicated with the many midcourse changes in the contract with the Russians and we had to make a whole bunch of new contracts.

It was decided that ISRO would develop in-house the control system to be used with the cryo engines. But the compatibility of the system had to be proven by actual tests with the Russian engines. A separate contract was made for this. Another one was made for the stage-level test since ISRO's facilities at Mahendragiri were not ready in time. The other major new contract with the Russians was for setting up the prelaunch propellant filling plants at SHAR. A contract was also concluded with Linde, Germany, for establishing a plant for the production of liquid hydrogen and oxygen at Mahendragiri.

These developments occurred over nearly a decade. Meanwhile, ISRO was buzzing with activity. We had regular successful launchings of PSLV. Some remote sensing satellites and INSATs were launched on foreign carriers since our own vehicles did not have the heavy payload capability.

The Russian cryostage went through a lot of back and forth discussions with the ISRO teams. They had to make sure it worked with the rest of the GSLV stages and the overall flight loads. The configuration of GSLV and its payload capability were also evolving. Finally, in 2001 when it was assembled on the SHAR launch pad, the GSLV had a satellite capability of 1540 kg in geosynchronous orbit, almost a tonne short of the original goal.

The vehicle that finally stood on the pad in March 2001 was a gigantic and complex one. The first or boost stage had a core solid propellant motor, 2.8 m in diameter loaded with 125 tonnes of propellant. It was surrounded by four liquid motors, 2 m in diameter, loaded with 40 tonnes of liquid propellant with their nozzles canted for aerodynamic stability. The solid core and the liquid strap-ons formed a single unit as the first stage. The second stage was the same as the PSLV second stage. The third stage was the cryostage built in Russia. The avionics packages and other mechanical and structural systems were of the same vintage as the PSLV with necessary modifications.

By this time I had retired and was not at a console but seated in the VIP gallery along with some of my senior colleagues. We were anxious observers waiting for the take-off scheduled for 28 March 2001. The prelaunch events were proceeding smoothly and the checks were satisfactory, which for a first launch was very commendable.

There were thousands of parameters to be constantly monitored prior to the launch and the checkout computers took over the countdown in what was termed the Automatic

Launch Sequence (ALS), minutes before the launch. The computers automatically stopped the counting if any parameter was found to deviate from the desired value so that the specialists could take remedial action.

R.V. Perumal, a man of immense experience and insight into launch vehicle technology, was the project director. Kasturirangan was still the ISRO chairman at that time and Madhavan Nair was director of VSSC. All of us were looking at the countdown clock for T-4 seconds when the four liquid strap-ons would ignite and reach a stable burn at the magic moment of T=0. That was when the solid booster was supposed to ignite. Then the monster of a rocket weighing 400 tonnes and with a height of 49 m would rise majestically out of the launch pad. The delay of about four seconds between the ignition of the liquid and solid stages was deliberate since it was necessary to have uniform burning of the four strap-ons before firing the larger solid stage. It is important to note that the liquid stage had a start–stop capability while the solid stage did not.

What followed was a rocket engineer's nightmare. At T=0, the giant vehicle did not lift off, since the core solid stage ignition command was aborted. The ALS system had automatically shut down the countdown a fraction of a second before the solid stage was to ignite! An aborted launch and that too of a rocket carrying various types of highly hazardous fuel! Now all the liquid and cryo propellants would have to be drained remotely and the stages dismantled. Extreme safety measures had to be taken for this. The process of returning to the launch mode was also a time consuming and cumbersome one.

There was panic and frustration all around. But it turned out not to be the catastrophic failure we had originally thought. A careful analysis later showed that it was actually a great stroke of good fortune that saved ISRO's day. The ground checkout computer had detected that one of the four strap-on engines was not burning with the full-rated thrust and this was not an acceptable condition for the flight. If it had taken off, the large vehicle would have had an unbalanced thrust, resulting in an uncontrolled flight path. If the solid stage had been allowed to fire it would have actually been catastrophic. The fact that the liquid stage could be shut off was actually a boon.

The telemetry data gathered during the crucial few seconds were scrutinized and analysed. The stages were carefully disassembled and the defective liquid engine was stripped for detailed inspection. And we found the culprit! One of the feed lines had a lump of lead blocking the flow of nitrogen tetroxide feeding the gas generator.

And how did the lead get in there? The hollow portions of these feed lines were filled with lead before they were beaten into shape. This is how they got the required bends to carry the gas within the engine. The lead was usually melted away after this was done. This particular piece must have escaped inspection and got into the assembly. We all remembered an incident which had occurred a few years ago when Ariane-4 launched by the ESA had had a similar launch failure because a strip of cotton cloth had blocked a feed line.

We soon realized that the first GSLV was an aborted launch and not a failure. Imagine the scenario if an identical problem had occurred in the second stage liquid engine of the vehicle which employed almost identical hardware. The ALS would have been out of the picture and the stage would have ignited and would not have developed any thrust, thus dumping the entire assembly into the sea. There would have been no hardware to inspect and we might never have detected the rather simple defect that caused the major disaster.

ISRO made a terrific comeback. Within three weeks the fresh assembly of GSLV with the corrected and certified hardware was on the launch pad, ready for another go. On 18 April 2001, at the second attempt, the vehicle successfully took off from the pad, this time with no interruption of the countdown. All the stages fired on time and the Russian cryostage put the GSAT-1 into an elliptical orbit.

While the performance of the lower stages was normal, the Russian stage did not perform to its full specifications and the orbit attained was shorter by 4000 km at the apogee. Much fuel meant for the spacecraft operations had to be wasted in raising the orbit to synchronous heights, which reduced the life of the satellite to about a year. It was, however, a great achievement for the ISRO community. They had demonstrated their ability to conceive and validate their design in an area of complex technology.

Over the next decade the GSLV programme continued involving both the cryostages bought from Russia and those using the indigenously developed ones. Continuous improvements were being made to increase the payload weight from the initial 1540 kg to 1800 kg or so.

Between 2003 and 2014, seven GSLV missions took off from SHAR. Four of them resulted in the successful orbiting of GSAT spacecraft. Three missions failed. Of these, two carried the Russian cryostages. The third failure was the GSLV-D3 launched in April 2010 carrying the first indigenous cryostage. The failures were due to a variety of causes. They were all carefully analysed and remedial action taken. Finally in January 2014, there was a great sense of triumph when GSLV-D5 carrying an indigenous cryostage performed flawlessly and delivered GSAT-14 into a synchronous transfer orbit.

15

From Rockets to Satellites

Right in the middle of a very tumultuous period, U.R. Rao retired, Kasturirangan took over as chairman, and I moved out of SHAR to become director of ISAC in Bangalore. However, I continued to be involved with the Sriharikota launch centre, which saw steady progress. There was a large-scale augmentation of facilities to tackle the GSLV launches. Larger solid boosters were being made. A variety of control centres and instrumentation complexes came up. All the facilities including logistics were enhanced to handle more frequent launchings. A state-of-the-art second launch pad was added for the simultaneous assembly of two vehicles so that launch frequencies could be increased. ISRO even began undertaking commercial launch services for other countries as the world-class infrastructure put in place now ensured a highly reliable delivery of launch services.

For me moving to ISAC in Bangalore was a refreshing change. ISAC was a very well-established centre by then and two of its directors had become chairmen of ISRO. I no longer had to run a township since the centre was in the middle of a big and throbbing city. More importantly, although I was certainly involved with the satellite programme right from its inception, I was basically a rocket man and this was going to be my first hands-on experience with building satellites.

The satellite programme had its origin in VSSC when U.R. Rao started the Satellite Systems Division (SSD) in 1969, two years before the death of Sarabhai. In the summer of 1971, the Soviet Union had offered to launch an Indian satellite into orbit. The Chinese put their first successful satellite into orbit in 1970 and this was perhaps the event which gave the Russian proposal a sudden new impetus. But when Sarabhai passed away in December 1971, everything was put on temporary hold.

M.G.K. Menon as chairman decided to take it forward. As a first move, he sanctioned the shifting of SSD to Bangalore. Rao located a site in the Peenya Industrial Area where some sheds were available and there India's first satellite project was born. By now Dhawan had taken charge. The first satellite project was designated as the Indo Soviet Satellite Project (ISSP). The first Indian satellite Aryabhata was an ISSP product.

Aryabhata was named after a fifth-century Indian mathematician and astronomer. It was a 360 kg spin-stabilized scientific satellite carrying X-ray astronomy, gamma rays and solar electron payloads. Rao's young and enthusiastic project team did an excellent job of building the spacecraft from scratch within the stipulated time. It was launched by the Soviet rocket Kosmas 3M from the Kapustin Yar launch base on 19 April 1975. It functioned well for about five days, but unfortunately lost power thereafter and the signals were lost.

The launch of Aryabhata heralded India's entry into the space era and marked the beginning of our very lively satellite programme. Aryabhata was followed by Bhaskara-1 in 1979 and Bhaskara-2 in 1981, both again launched by Soviet rockets. Both satellites carried remote sensing payloads and were the precursors to the constellation of remote sensing payloads to be launched with PSLV in later years. Next came the INSAT series.

The first few INSATs were built by Ford Aerospace in the US, and launched from American rockets. I went to Palo Alto with a big ISRO team for the mission readiness review of the Insat-1A which was launched by a Delta launcher in April 1982. Following a series of failures, the satellite was abandoned in September 1983, less than eighteen months into a seven-year mission.

Just like with our rockets, we went through a learning curve with our satellites too. But, by the time I took over ISAC our satellite programme was doing very well and we were building much bigger and more complex satellites which now provided our country with a neural network of communication. ISAC had grown into a large organization and moved into a modern and well-planned campus near the old Bangalore airport, on land adjoining the National Aeronautical Laboratory (NAL). We had built and launched large satellites such as APPLE, which was launched under an agreement with ESA, and communication satellites in the INSAT-1 series. As the indigenous launch vehicle programme progressed ISAC built the satellites such as RS-D1, RS-D2, SROSS series, IRS series and the INSAT indigenous series.

The spacecraft built at ISAC were launched by a variety of launch vehicles. In India we used the ASLV, PSLV and GSLV. But we also used international launch vehicles for heavier satellites launched from launch bases at Kourou in French Guiana and Baikonur in Kazakhstan. In the early years even the American Space Shuttle was used to launch our satellite. The launch vehicle was identified depending on the weight of the spacecraft and its proposed orbit.

ISAC was particularly stretched to its limits during my tenure. We built and launched a total of seven spacecraft during the three and a half years I spent there. SROSS-C2 was launched using ASLV while IRS-P2, IRS-P3 and IRS-1D were launched by PSLV. INSAT-2C and INSAT-D were launched from Kourou by Ariane rockets and IRS-1C from Baikonur using a Russian rocket.

The transportation of a fully built satellite to the launch site is a highly complex and delicate task. Special environmentally controlled containers have to be designed to ensure that the spacecraft are protected from the mechanical and thermal shocks experienced during transportation. If the launch is from SHAR, the prime mover vehicles have to be carefully chosen and the road transportation takes place under the heavy escort and surveillance of local authorities. In case the launch is from French Guiana or Baikonur, large cargo aircraft have to be chartered to directly and exclusively fly our precious cargo to the nearest airport. Many such sorties have been carried out over the years without any mishaps.

Although I had personally been involved in several satellite launch missions at Sriharikota, I had never actually taken part in one such mission at a foreign launch station until I became director of ISAC. I was therefore really looking forward to my first experience in 1995 when we went to Kourou for the INSAT-2C launch. As a rocket specialist I was interested in seeing how they had managed to streamline their launch activities so well that now they launched satellites with a kind of assembly line precision. As the director of ISAC, I was directly responsible for the satellite we were about to launch and I had to make sure that all systems were ready to go.

After my first visit in 1970, I had gone to Kourou a few more times to attend conferences. But this time it was special: For the first time, I was going to oversee the launch of our own satellite, INSAT-2C. The spacecraft had already been flown to Cayenne, the airport nearest to Kourou, and had been taken from there to the launch base by road, more than a month in advance. I reached Kourou along with ISRO Chairman Kasturirangan and some others after a long and tiring flight from Paris. The project team was in the process of completing the assembly and testing of the spacecraft a few days before the scheduled launch date. This time too I stayed in the Hotel Des Roches.

Kourou, like SHAR, is an equatorial launch site. Its location on the northern shore of South America makes it an ideal site for both equatorial and polar launches. The Atlantic Ocean provides a vast safety zone for both types of missions. By the 1990s, Arianespace, the commercial wing of ESA, had streamlined launches on payment for customers from all over the world. Right from keeping accounts for the various services provided to the customer to the meticulous countdown of events, things progressed like clockwork.

By now the Kourou launch station commanded about 50 per cent of the space transportation market. It had successfully orbited 127 satellites. In 1995 alone Arianespace had made a profit of 190 million French francs. From a meagre ten orders in 1981, the numbers had grown rapidly and soon there was a backlog of satellites waiting to be launched. In fact, to get a ride on an Ariane rocket, the customer had to book years ahead. Rocket launchings at Kourou now took place with clockwork efficiency.

India was one of Arianespace's oldest customers. APPLE, one of India's oldest satellites, was launched from French Guiana in 1981. Over the intervening years a couple of INSATs had been launched and many more were scheduled to go up from here. We were now entering the big league and playing with the giants. Our INSAT's co-passengers on the Ariane launches were often huge communication satellites from the US and other international agencies. We had certainly come a long way.

At Kourou ISRO was a respected long-time friend and I realized our teams were quite at home here. As usual, various groups from ISAC had been moving up and down from Kourou for nearly a month by now. While a core team of senior persons was there right through, groups of others handling subsystems, assembly and so on spent a couple of weeks whenever required. Since some of them were veterans at Kourou launches, they had even brought provisions from India and set up kitchens.

The Indian satellite teams were well settled in their assigned areas for their work, and the testing and integration of the satellite to the Ariane vehicle took place smoothly. As the launch window neared we assumed our positions in the consoles and carefully monitored the status of the rocket and the spacecraft. The take-off was perfect and our satellite was injected into the correct orbit.

It was a unique experience, waiting for the message from the Indian tracking station halfway across the globe at Hassan in Karnataka. Within minutes we got our thumbs up. They had spotted and locked on to the spacecraft.

It was now celebration time! The next evening Arianespace threw a cocktail and dinner party. The Indian team, not to be outdone, pooled all its resources and prepared a grand Indian dinner for the range staff.

When Sarabhai had dreamed of having our own communication satellites so we could 'leapfrog' into the future, he could not have imagined that his baby would one day be holding its own in such big company. Building technologically advanced satellites, transporting them across thousands of miles, loading them on to launchers, manoeuvring them into orbit and taking care of them for years, required scientific skill of a very high order. And we had proved once again that we could do it.

The work of the Indian team, however, had just started. We had to perform further operations on the spacecraft to see that it was manoeuvred into a geosynchronous orbit before the payloads were turned on. This could only be done from Hassan. The concerned project team had to rush to India and reach Hassan by the time the spacecraft appeared at their location. The process of coaxing the satellite into the correct slot and carefully operationalizing the payloads would take a few weeks, and it would take some more time before the transponders could be allotted to the users.

By now most of our launches were telecast and we had proud and eager audiences watching us from all over the country. The Kourou launch too was covered by the Indian and international media, and our families back at home could share the sweetness of our success.

But for me there was more in store in the next couple of weeks. From the humid pressure cooker climes of French Guiana, I had to fly to the bone-chilling cold of Kazakhstan. Shortly after I returned to Bangalore I had to get ready to fly to Russia for our next mission. This would be my second experience of launching a satellite from a foreign country. I used to joke that we were being 'tempered' by going through a 'hot and cold' treatment. Certainly it was no joke to go within a couple of weeks from the coastal climate in French Guiana to the temperate Bangalore winter and then plunge directly into ice-bound Baikonur, Kazakhstan.

It was December 1995. I was making my second trip to Moscow that year. The first one was when I had gone with a group of ISAC engineers in January that year to finalize the details of the Russian contract to launch IRS-1C on a Molniya rocket. I was the head of the delegation then and spent most of the time in negotiations with the Russians.

Since that was my first trip to Moscow I took some time off for a brief tour. I visited the Kremlin and got a glimpse of the embalmed and fresh-looking body of Lenin. It was winter and Moscow was snowbound. On the second trip in December for the actual launch campaign I was accompanied by Kasturirangan.

The situation was pretty bad in Russia then and our team members who had been there a couple of times before had fortified themselves with food and medicines. I was beginning to realize why the Russian scientists who came to India never wanted to leave Trivandrum or Sriharikota! They loved the balmy weather. They were also housed in extremely comfortable guest houses with food, transport and entertainment readily available. And all this was in the 1990s, at a time when in Russia even essentials came at a premium.

The Soviet Union was collapsing and life was pretty tough for the Russians. The once mighty academicians were almost on the streets. There was no money, no jobs and the rouble was hitting rock-bottom. In the eyes of the Russians we Indians were the rich and well-to-do.

The launch of IRS-1C was scheduled for 29 December. I had fortified myself with plenty of what I thought was warm clothing. But my Russian colleagues took one look at it and shook their heads sadly. Nothing was adequate. The Russians had come to meet us prepared with a complete set of winter outer garments. We were warned that the winter in Baikonur was harsher than in Moscow and even our shoes were of no use. We were all given a fresh set of heavy snowshoes. Soon

I was wrapped up in heavy Russian furs and wore warm woollen headgear. I am a tall man. Fortunately the Russians were big built and they could find clothes which fitted me!

The distance between Moscow and Baikonur was about 2100 km and the flight took two and a half hours. Actually, by that time Kazakhstan, where Baikonur was located, was an independent nation but the cosmodrome itself was still under Russian control. This was the famous cosmodrome from which many satellites, including all their manned flights, were launched. Yuri Gagarin had been launched into space from here.

The only feasible route to travel from Moscow to Baikonur was by air. Our flight was fully booked. The passengers were an assorted lot including engineers like us and Kazakhs of all description. There were even some sturdy rural folk in their ethnic wear lugging all kinds of things including birds and animals! There was a long line in the tarmac waiting to board the aircraft. The passengers were finally packed into the plane and we took off. It was obviously a low-cost flight and we had to buy our own food and beverage. Since we had no low-cost flights in India those days it was a new experience.

We arrived at Baikonur airport and were taken to our modest hotel. Academician Duneyev, the coordinator of our mission, threw us a dinner party for which he collected money from us at the end! It was freezing cold. We spent the night trying to keep warm in our inadequately heated rooms.

The next day we were driven to the Cosmodrome where the satellite was being prepared. Clad in our special Russian winter wear, we travelled for almost an hour by bus through snow-covered deserts. One car was hired for the senior Indian officials, but the Russian chief had to thumb a ride with us because he could not afford to hire one for himself!

The Baikonur launch base was desert-like. The IRS satellite had already been flown to Baikonur from Bangalore by a chartered Ilyushin aircraft; our advanced team was at work; the mating of the satellite to the rocket was in progress. Young soldiers in uniform, obviously thoroughly trained in rocket assembly operations, were going about their work with military precision. Their leader barked out commands and they reacted as though they were in a drill. The thought occurred to me that they might be routinely launching rockets or maybe even missiles in their hundreds. The Russian rocket programme was, after all, an offshoot of their missile programme.

I noticed another peculiarity. Unlike in the West, all rocket work in Russia is carried out on rail tracks. The giant rockets and their launchers are conveyed on tracks right up to the pad. This, too, was because of the missile programme. In Russia, quick transportation of missiles across long distances by railway was paramount to their preparedness. The same tracks were used for launching rockets as well. Also, Russian launch stations were situated not next to the sea but in the middle of vast deserts. The debris landed in the huge empty expanses.

Ours was a morning launch. We had assembled at the rocket preparation area. Soon the rocket with the assembled satellite was ready to be moved to the launch pad. The Russians had their own tradition for launching their rockets.

As soon as it was ready to be moved, all of us gathered behind the carriage transporting the rocket. As the rocket moved slowly along the tracks towards the pad we followed behind on foot almost as though in a wedding procession! After that we walked back to the assembly building to watch further preparations prior to launch.

As we walked back, I remembered our own traditions back home in India. Before a satellite or rocket was moved from Bangalore or Trivandrum, there would be a small puja, usually performed by one of our own personnel assuming the garb of a priest. Similarly, before the MST tower was moved, a coconut was broken. And finally, before every major launch, the chairman of the time would make a quick trip to Tirupati, which is quite close to Sriharikota, carrying models of the rocket and spacecraft, in order to receive the blessings of Balaji. On the day of the launch everyone would troop to the temple in Sriharikota and pray for its success.

To witness the take-off at Baikonur, we were herded into a tent erected in the middle of the desert at a spot the Russians considered safe from falling stages or even a stage gone astray. At one point I wondered how they would launch that huge rocket under what looked like totally primitive conditions.

But I need not have worried. The Russians were veterans and the launch itself went off with great precision. It was a surreal atmosphere as we stood there in the tent in what seemed like the middle of nowhere, waiting for the take-off. There was a van with a TV crew covering the launch and relaying the images to Doordarshan in India in real time. The countdown proceeded and the majestic rocket took off.

The performance of the vehicle was flawless and our IRS spacecraft was injected into the correct orbit.

Back home everyone sat glued to the TV sets, excited at the prospect of watching an Indian-made satellite zoom into space atop a Russian rocket. Everything was happening across the globe and they were getting to watch it from their own homes. My eighty-two-year-old mother had especially told me that she and my father would be watching and that I should make some sign to indicate to her that I remembered. So, as we stood there in the icy cold with snow all around us responding to the TV anchor, I lifted my hand and waved. My mother, I later heard, was thrilled and waved back to me. She boasted later to all her neighbours and friends that her son had waved to her from the middle of a Russian desert!

16
Using Space Technology

The Space Applications Centre (SAC) in Ahmedabad was the only one of the four main ISRO centres in which I had not actually worked during my thirty-five-year stint in ISRO.

SAC was created in 1972 after Sarabhai passed away. All the space application activities of ISRO, which were largely located in Ahmedabad, were consolidated here with the eminent scientist Yash Pal as the director. Its mandate was to develop capabilities to use space technology for earth observation, satellite communication, disaster management, navigation and the study of climate and environment.

But space applications had been on the agenda from the very inception of our space programme. Sarabhai loved to use the term 'leapfrog'. He would tell us that we in India should use the latest technology, such as atomic energy and space, to 'leapfrog' into a developed society. He often told us, for instance, that if we used satellites for TV broadcast, we could simply bypass the land-based transmission lines which he said would soon be obsolete. And he said this at a time when we didn't have TV transmission even in our major cities! He wanted TV to reach the remotest villages, not for entertainment but because he thought it was the quickest way to spread education and awareness.

So, even while he was setting up TERLS he initiated parallel planning for the development of space technology and its application for national growth. In fact, he did not even want to wait for India's own satellites with payloads for various applications. He initiated experimental work using foreign satellites in order to give us a feel for the type of work that could be carried out. He also wanted to see how TV could be used as a tool for spreading awareness. It is interesting that one of the earliest telecasts was *Krishi Darshan*, a TV programme on agricultural information for farmers.

Sarabhai was convinced that space technology had the potential to address the real problems of man and society. As the director of PRL he assembled an army of able and brilliant scientists, anthropologists, communicators and social scientists from all corners of the country to spearhead the Indian space programme.

In 1967, the first Experimental Satellite Communication Earth Station (ESCES), located in Ahmedabad, was operationalized. This doubled as a training centre for Indian as well as international scientists and engineers. Next came the Satellite Instructional Television Experiment (SITE), hailed as 'the largest sociological experiment in the world'. Although Sarabhai had initiated this as well, by the time it became a reality in 1975, he had passed away. ATS-6, an

American satellite, was used for beaming development-oriented programmes created in India for rural audiences. About 200,000 people living in 2400 villages in six states were covered; 50,000 science teachers in primary schools benefitted from this programme which lasted a year.

SITE was followed by the Satellite Telecommunication Experiments Project (STEP), a joint project of ISRO and the Post and Telegraphs Department (P&T) using the Franco-German Symphonie satellite. This lasted for two years from 1977 to 1979. STEP did for telecommunication experiments what SITE did for TV experiments. There was also a programme for airborne remote sensing in Kerala for studying large-scale coconut diseases. All these programmes were to help potential users to develop a feel for the possibilities of use of space technology for solving national problems.

Later, as we started building our own satellites, space application became very central to our programme. By 1980, another application unit was added to our ISRO family. The National Remote Sensing Agency (NRSA) at Hyderabad, which was set up in 1974 under the Department of Science and Technology, came under the Department of Space in 1980. This was where the earth observation data was processed and disseminated to users. Various government and other user agencies were also trained and encouraged to utilize the data obtained.

Being basically a rocket and ground systems specialist, my association with SAC was not very close until I was asked by Satish Dhawan to look at the quality and reliability practices all across ISRO. That was when I started working with the R&QA personnel at SAC. I was able to initiate some standardization of practices, especially where inter-centre projects were involved.

When I became the director of ISAC I had occasion to interact more intensely with the payload development teams of SAC as they were building subsystems for satellites integrated at ISAC. Satellite payloads like communication transponders, high-resolution space-based CCD cameras and a variety of space-based sensors were built at SAC. For years now, these have been successfully flown in various satellites and are functioning very satisfactorily. Over the years a number of communication satellites have been launched and operated by ISRO. Space communication is now taken for granted in India. In this area at least, we have truly realized Sarabhai's dream and leapfrogged into the future. I don't know how many people realize that we never had a widespread terrestrial TV network. Instead we jumped straight into the space age!

The Direct to Home (DTH) commercial services provided by data received from our satellites are now extensively used for telemedicine and tele-education apart from entertainment. Very Small Aperture Terminals (VSAT) are used particularly for disaster management and other emergency communications. They also have national defence uses.

The IRS spacecraft have provided reliable and timely information to various user agencies on the state of the land, ocean and atmosphere. They have also enabled effective planning and efficient deployment of resources for their optimum management. In fact, ISRO helps neighbouring countries in this area. Under the National Natural Resources Management System (NNRMS), all the ISRO centres including the state level Regional Remote Sensing Centres (RRSCs) ensure the proper dissemination and prompt utilization of space information.

Today, our satellites form our country's neural network. We have gone far beyond Sarabhai's mandate and now process and use our own voluminous satellite data for a mind-boggling array of things. We take our satellites for granted. Imagine what would have happened if we were still dependent on countries who could just block us out on a whim.

17

The Way We Work

The Brahm Prakash Hall at SHAR brims with engineers shuffling their data sheets and reports. They speak excitedly to each other about their subsystems. To a stranger, however technically advanced, their exchanges sound like Greek and Latin, riddled with acronyms and jargon. Only the assembly of 400-odd engineers can understand each other perfectly.

The Mission Readiness Review (MRR) is in session. We are just a few days away from a major launch campaign. Each of the engineers responsible for a particular subsystem is getting ready to go on stage and present details of the tests carried out on it. Problems, solutions, tests, last-minute tweaks – everything is covered.

The group is an amazing mix of veterans and greenhorns and everyone in between. Anyone who is part of the project and has something to say is there. I sit next to the chairman and senior centre directors. Retired pioneers like me who are experienced experts in certain fields form an integral part of the MRR. To the newest recruit attending an MRR for the first time it is a thrilling and challenging experience.

As one of the senior engineers finishes his presentation, a voice from the last row raises an issue. It is a junior engineer. There is absolute silence as everyone in the room gives him a patient hearing. The engineer who is making the presentation takes notes and gives a detailed response. It really does not matter that the questioner is quite junior in the hierarchy, for in that hall there is absolute technical democracy and no voice is stifled. Everyone knows that many an important issue has come to light at an MRR and at times major failures have been averted because someone raised a pertinent question.

The MRR epitomizes the functioning of ISRO, where the work ethics had evolved over the years. Democracy has always been the key word. Every issue raised is analysed and addressed with utmost seriousness. This in turn has yielded results which are unique and unusual in a government-run scientific department.

Homi Bhabha, the innovator who changed the bureaucratic style of running scientific organizations, made sure that scientists determined their own policies. He also insisted that they were the administrative heads of their organizations and were answerable only to the prime minister. ISRO under Sarabhai followed the same path, with more procedural innovations suited to the unforgiving nature of space technology.

Openness has been the hallmark of ISRO in all its activities. The MRR is just one example. Whether it is in the planning process or long-term goals definition, budget formulation or progress reviews, design reviews, quality and reliability assessment, recruitment or promotion of personnel, transparency has always played a vital role.

Because of its strategic nature, space technology is closely guarded by its creators. ISRO therefore had to develop its own technology from scratch with a great deal of trial and error. But our results have always been open for free scrutiny by the public. Failures and successes in our field are splashed across the sky for all to see. Our major missions are conducted in the full glare of live media spotlight and the world can learn in real time of our success or failure.

Today, we are no longer a mere handful of engineers experimenting with sounding rockets. The annual budget of the organization was a few lakhs of rupees in 1963. This has grown to several thousand crores. ISRO has more than 20,000 employees. In fact, we are now seriously trying not to add to the numbers by transferring repetitive work to the industry.

But most importantly, ISRO has built a strong and confident human resource pool ready to take on many more challenges. Advanced countries have recognized that ISRO is on par with many developed countries in the field of space technology. And we achieved this by ourselves, on a shoestring budget. The average Indian is proud of ISRO's achievements and that means a lot to us.

Our centres are seamlessly filled with fresh technical personnel every decade without any discontinuity of the programmes. Most of the technical manpower is drawn from graduates from all over the country who come from lesser-known institutions. And many of these engineers and scientists have turned out to be outstanding leaders in their own fields.

By the late 1990s, when the IT boom in the country hit our programmes, our young recruits were lured away with fat salaries. But the trend reversed when the government revised its salaries upwards and offered lifelong perks which could never be matched by the IT firms. More importantly, ISRO still had exciting programmes compared to the mind-numbing jobs the software companies had to offer. Slowly the young people began to trickle back.

Around that time I was asked by the then chairman, Kasturirangan, to tour the ISRO centres and talk to the scientists and engineers, particularly the young ones, to find out what they felt about their work environment. I visited all the centres and spoke to them about their joys and frustrations, and asked them what needed to be done to keep them at ISRO.

Two surprising findings came through. One, that they all were quite happy with their assignments and the visibility of the overall goals of the organization vis-à-vis their contributions. Two, the salary differences between ISRO and the private organizations did not bother them as much as we had feared. Their complaints were more mundane ones about the non-availability of high-speed internet connections and access to PCs. We were able to tackle these issues quite easily over the next couple of months.

ISRO today is often held up as an example of a particularly well-run and result-oriented government organization.

How did this happen? One factor which plays a crucial role is careful planning. ISRO has always defined profiles of planned activities a decade ahead after due consultations with the general scientific and planning community. These activities are directly linked to utilization and national development. The profile is finalized and presented to the government of the day for approval in principle. Once the broad plan is approved, it is disseminated to the engineers and scientists down to the latest recruit. They in turn prepare detailed plans and projects with proper cost estimates. After a thorough scrutiny of all the proposals, a request for funding is made to the government.

At the very outset the potential users of information are identified and sometimes even trained in the use of the results. The capacities are created after setting goals. This applies, for example, to the remote sensed imagery and the use of transponders. Reliability and quality norms are set in advance and monitored by full-time teams throughout the course of the programmes. These norms also apply to the industrial partners and other agencies associated with the projects. Above all, there is absolute transparency right through, from the development phase to the final missions. Experts can always apply mid-course corrections. Of course, the bottom line is that ISRO's missions are such that the final missions are broadcast live to the public across the skies!

The ISRO family has considerable job satisfaction because we can see for ourselves the application of our contribution to national development. We have even been able to monetize our products even though we are not a commercial organization. For example, today, products and services including satellite launch services are made available to national and international users on a commercial basis through ISRO's commercial arm, the Antrix Corporation.

By 2015, within a short span of forty-odd years, ISRO had built and launched seventy-two satellites of increasing complexities. Our own remote sensing satellites, communication satellites and science satellites circled the earth in polar and geosynchronous orbits. The Chandrayaan moon mission and the Mars Orbiter Mission caught the imagination of the nation. The capability of ISRO in the satellite-building area rivalled that of the most advanced countries of the world and the data from the satellites were in demand internationally

Side by side, by 2015 more than twenty-five successful launches of PSLV had taken place successively, setting a kind of international record. With regular improvements in performance and optimization, the payload capacity increased from 1000 kg to about 1850 kg, depending on the choice of configuration.

The PSLV vehicle, now internationally recognized as a highly reliable and cost-effective rocket, is much sought-after by various countries for launching their remote sensing satellites into sun synchronous polar orbits. Variants of PSLV launched the lunar mission, the Mars Orbiter Mission and even a small GSAT synchronous satellite. Our own fleet of remote-sensing satellites is also performing excellently. And so are the large INSAT communication spacecraft orbited aboard Ariane rockets.

By this time so many chairmen have come and gone – Sarabhai, M.G.K. Menon, Dhawan, U.R. Rao, Kasturirangan, Madhavan Nair and Radhakrishnan – and not once was there a glitch in the programme because the man at the helm had changed. In 2015 at a GSLV launch when an important Indian-made cryostage proved its worth, I realized something exciting. Almost every single person at the helm, right from the ISRO chairman down to the mission director, was new! They had all assumed charge just a few months before.

Kiran Kumar, former director of SAC, was chairman. Sivan, former project director of GSLV, was the director of VSSC, Somnath was the new director of LPSC and Kunhi Krishnan had just taken over SHAR. They were all ISRO veterans who had come up through the system. I was amazed at the confidence and quiet competence with which they handled this complex launch.

Watching them work made me proud once more of the ISRO family to which I belonged.

Although I formally retired from ISRO in 1997, my close, almost umbilical connection with the organization can never be severed. I still sit in on important reviews and meetings, and continue to keep track of all the developments.

On a visit to SHAR in 2015, for instance, I was impressed by the dramatic augmentation in certain areas like the solid booster production plant. The huge boosters being manufactured there had no comparison to the tiny ones used for the SLV back in the 1980s. Similarly, I felt proud to see our state-of-the-art launch towers zooming high above the SHAR treeline and recalled the basic rail launcher we had used for our SLV launches. We were now handling almost one complex launch a month from SHAR whereas just twenty-five years ago we were launching once in two or three years.

By 2015 ISAC had also heavily augmented its capability to build and launch bigger and more sophisticated spacecraft. The numbers had substantially increased. An additional facility for testing the spacecraft under various electrical and environmental conditions had been built a short distance away from the main ISAC campus. Under one large roof we now have a world-class network of complex and expensive facilities to integrate and qualify a spacecraft.

Manned missions, bigger rockets, more complex satellites, assembly line launches… when the sky is no longer the limit, anything is possible.

Epilogue

I have grown along with ISRO, from the days when it was a mere idea in a visionary's mind through its phenomenal transformation in more than half a century into the veritable giant it is today. I have seen successive leaders steering it through its exciting phases almost seamlessly. Technical expertise and leadership have sprung from its workforce, as if by magic, to carry the torch forward. Failures have been converted to rich learning experiences followed by eventual triumphs.

I have sat in the control rooms with accelerating heartbeats when bold new missions like the Chandrayaan or Mangalyaan had taken off and shared the exhilaration among the colleagues when the missions succeeded. I have watched the politicians of the day proudly acclaiming ISRO's feats nationally and internationally almost as if those were their own achievements. I have gleefully noted the reluctant acceptance of ISRO's achievements by the advanced countries who were unwilling to share their know-how with us. And I enjoy watching many foreign agencies vying with each other for rides on our rockets!

And we are nowhere near the end of the story. ISRO has many more exciting milestones to cross in the forthcoming years. We still have to perfect a heavy lift cryogenic-powered workhorse vehicle. We have to send out missions with humans and recover them. We need to send more missions into deep space to explore new frontiers.

I am hoping to see some of these triumphs in my lifetime and have no doubt that ISRO will grow from strength to strength to meet these challenges, and more.

Annexure 1

Milestones

1962

- Indian National Committee for Space Research (INCOSPAR) formed and work on establishing Thumba Equatorial Rocket Launching Station (TERLS) started

1963

- First sounding rocket launch from TERLS (21 November)

1965

- Space Science and Technology Centre (SSTC) established in Thumba

1967

- Experimental Satellite Communication Earth Station (ESCES) set up at Ahmedabad

1968

- TERLS dedicated to the United Nations (2 February)

1969
- Indian Space Research Organisation (ISRO) formed (15 August)

1972
- Space Commission and Department of Space (DOS) set up. ISRO brought under DOS (1 June)

1972–76
- Airborne remote sensing experiments

1975
- ISRO becomes a government organization (1 April)
- First Indian satellite, Aryabhata, launched (19 April)

1975–76
- Satellite Instructional Television Experiment (SITE) conducted

1977–79
- Satellite Telecommunication Experimental Project (STEP) carried out

1979
- Bhaskara-I, an experimental satellite for earth observations, launched (7 June)
- First experimental launch of Satellite Launch Vehicle SLV-3 with Rohini Technology Payload (RTP) on board (10 August). Satellite could not be placed in orbit

1980

- Second experimental launch of SLV-3 (18 July). Rohini satellite successfully placed in orbit

1981

- First developmental launch of SLV-3. RS-D1 placed in orbit (31 May)
- APPLE, an experimental geostationary communication satellite, successfully launched (19 June)
- Bhaskara-II launched (20 November)

1982

- Indian National Satellite System 1A (INSAT-1A) launched (10 April). Deactivated on 6 September 1982

1983

- Second developmental launch of SLV-3. RS-D2 placed in orbit (17 April)
- INSAT-1B launched (30 August)

1984

- Indo-Soviet manned space mission (April)

1987

- First developmental launch of Augmented Satellite Launch Vehicle (ASLV) with SROSS-1 satellite on board (24 March). Satellite could not be placed in orbit

1988
- Launch of first operational Indian Remote Sensing (IRS) satellite, IRS-1A (17 March)
- Second developmental launch of ASLV with SROSS-2 on board (13 July). Satellite could not be placed in orbit
- INSAT-1C launched (22 July). Abandoned in November 1989

1990
- INSAT-1D launched (12 June)

1991
- Launch of second operational remote sensing satellite, IRS-1B (29 August)

1992
- Third developmental launch of ASLV with SROSS-C on board (20 May). Satellite placed in orbit
- INSAT-2A, the first satellite of the indigenously built second-generation INSAT series, launched (10 July)

1993
- INSAT-2B, the second satellite in INSAT-2 series, launched (23 July)
- PSLV-D1, the first developmental launch of the Polar Satellite Launch Vehicle (PSLV), with IRS-1E on board (20 September). Satellite could not be placed in orbit

1994

- Fourth developmental launch of ASLV with SROSS-C2 on board (4 May). Satellite placed in orbit
- PSLV-D2, the second developmental launch of PSLV, with IRS-P2 on board (15 October). Satellite successfully placed in polar sun synchronous orbit

1995

- INSAT-2C, the third satellite in INSAT-2 series, launched (7 December)
- Launch of third operational Indian remote sensing satellite, IRS-1C (28 December)

1996

- PSLV-D3, the third developmental launch of PSLV, with IRS-P3 on board (21 March). Satellite placed in polar sun synchronous orbit

1997

- INSAT-2D, fourth satellite in INSAT-2 series, launched (4 June). Becomes inoperable on 4 October 1997. (An in-orbit satellite, ARABSAT-1C, later renamed INSAT-2DT, was acquired in November 1997 to partly augment the INSAT system)
- PSLV-C1, the first operational launch of PSLV, with IRS-1D on board (29 September). Satellite placed in orbit

1998

- INSAT system capacity augmented with the readiness of INSAT-2DT acquired from ARABSAT (January)

1999

- INSAT-2E, the last satellite in the multipurpose INSAT-2 series, launched by Ariane from Kourou, French Guiana (3 April)
- Indian remote sensing satellite, IRS-P4 (OCEANSAT-1), launched by PSLV-C2 along with Korean KITSAT-3 and German DLR-TUBSAT from SHAR centre, Sriharikota (26 May)

2000

- INSAT-3B, the first satellite in the third generation INSAT-3 series, launched by Ariane from Kourou, French Guiana (22 March)

2001

- Successful flight test of Geosynchronous Satellite Launch Vehicle (GSLV-D1) on 18 April with an experimental satellite GSAT-1 on board
- Successful launch of PSLV-C3 on 22 October placing three satellites – India's TES, Belgian PROBA and German BIRD – into polar sun synchronous orbit

2002

- Successful launch of INSAT-3C by Ariane from Kourou, French Guiana (24 January)
- Successful launch of KALPANA-1 by ISRO's PSLV-C4 from SDSC SHAR (12 September)

2003

- Successful launch of INSAT-3A by Ariane from Kourou, French Guiana (10 April)
- GSLV-D2, the second developmental test flight of GSLV, with GSAT-2 on board successfully launched from SDSC SHAR (8 May)
- Successful launch of INSAT-3E by Ariane from Kourou, French Guiana (28 September)
- Successful launch of RESOURCESAT-1 by ISRO's PSLV-C5 from SDSC SHAR (17 October)

2004

- GSLV-F01, the first operational flight of GSLV, with GSAT-3 (also known as EDUSAT) on board launched from SDSC SHAR (20 September). EDUSAT successfully placed in Geosynchronous Transfer Orbit (GTO)

2005

- Successful launch of CARTOSAT-1 and HAMSAT by PSLV-C6 from the newly established second launch pad at SDSC SHAR (5 May)
- Successful launch of INSAT-4A by Ariane from Kourou, French Guiana (22 December)

2006

- GSLV-F02, the second operational flight of GSLV, from SDSC SHAR with INSAT-4C on board (10 July). The satellite could not be placed in orbit

2007

- PSLV-C7 successfully launches four satellites – India's CARTOSAT-2 and Space Capsule Recovery Experiment (SRE-1) as well as Indonesia's LAPAN-TUBSAT and Argentina's PEHUENSAT-1 (10 January)
- Successful recovery of SRE-1 after manoeuvring it to re-enter the earth's atmosphere and descend over the Bay of Bengal about 140 km east of Sriharikota (22 January)
- Successful launch of INSAT-4B by Ariane from Korou, French Guiana (12 March)
- PSLV-C8 successfully launches an Italian satellite AGILE under a commercial contract with Antrix Corporation (23 April)
- Launch of GSLV-F04 with INSAT-4CR on board from SDSC SHAR (2 September)

2008

- PSLV-C10 successfully launches TECSAR satellite under a commercial contract with Antrix Corporation (21 January)
- PSLV-C9 successfully launches ten satellites – India's CARTOSAT-2A, Indian Mini Satellite-1 (IMS-1) and eight Nano Satellites for International Customers under a commercial contract with Antrix Corporation (28 April)
- PSLV-C11 successfully launches Chandrayaan-1 (22 October)
- Ariane-5 launch vehicle successfully launches W2M satellite jointly built by Antrix/ISRO and EADS Astrium on a commercial basis (21 December)

2009

- PSLV-C12 successfully launches RISAT-2 and ANUSAT (20 April)
- PSLV-C14 successfully launches OCEANSAT-2 and six nanosatellites for international customers under a commercial contract with Antrix Corporation (23 September)

2010

- Successful static testing of GSLV-Mk III launch vehicle's S200 solid propellant booster rocket stage (24 January)
- GSLV-D3, the first launch of GSLV with indigenous cryogenic upper stage and GSAT-4 satellite on-board (15 April). GSAT-4 could not be placed in orbit
- PSLV-C15, the seventeenth flight of PSLV, successfully launches India's CARTOSAT-2B and STUDSAT, Algeria's ALSAT-2A, Canada's NLS-1 and NLS-2 (12 July)
- Successful static testing of GSLV-Mk III launch vehicle's L110 liquid core stage (8 September)
- European Ariane-5 launch vehicle successfully launches HYLAS satellite jointly built by Antrix/ISRO and EADS Astrium on a commercial basis (27 November)
- GSLV-F06, the seventh launch of GSLV with GSAT-5P satellite on-board (25 December), could not place the satellite in orbit

2011

- PSLV-C16 successfully launches India's RESOURCESAT–2, YOUTHSAT and X-SAT from Singapore (20 April)

- GSAT-8 communication satellite launched by Ariane from Kourou, French Guiana (21 May)
- PSLV-C17 successfully launches GSAT-12 communication satellite (15 July)
- Second successful static testing of S-200 booster to be used in GSLV-Mk III (4 September)
- PSLV-C18 successfully launches the Indo-French satellite Megha-Tropiques and three co-passenger satellites – Jugnu from IIT, Kanpur, SRMSat from SRM University, Chennai, and VesselSat–1 from Luxembourg (12 October)

2012

- PSLV, in its twenty-first flight (PSLV-C19), launches India's first Radar Imaging Satellite (RISAT-1) from SHAR (26 April)
- In its twenty-second flight (PSLV-C21), PSLV successfully launches French earth observation satellite SPOT-6 along with Japanese micro-satellite PROITERES from SHAR (9 September)
- India's heaviest communication satellite, GSAT-10, successfully launched by Ariane-5 VA-209 from Kourou, French Guiana (29 September)

2013

- PSLV, in its twenty-third flight (PSLV-C20), successfully launches Indo-French Satellite SARAL along with six smaller satellites from SHAR (25 February)

- PSLV, in its twenty-fourth flight (PSLV-C22), successfully launches India's first dedicated navigational satellite IRNSS-1A from SHAR (1 July)
- India's advanced weather satellite INSAT-3D successfully launched by Ariane-5 VA-214 from Kourou, French Guiana (26 July)
- India's advanced communication satellite GSAT-7 successfully launched by Ariane-5 VA-215 from Kourou, French Guiana (30 August)
- Mars Orbiter Mission, the India's first interplanetary mission to planet Mars, successfully launched by PSLV-C25 from SHAR (5 November)
- Trans-Mars injection manoeuvre performed on Mars Orbiter spacecraft to place it in Mars transfer trajectory (1 December)

2014
- GSLV-D5 carrying indigenous cryogenic upper stage successfully places GSAT-14 into GTO (5 January)
- GSLV D5/GSAT 14 launched successfully from SHAR (5 January)
- PSLV C24/IRNSS-1B successfully launched (4 April)
- PSLV C23/SPOT-7 successfully launched with co-passengers A SAT, NLS7.1, NLS 7.2 and VELOX 1 (30 June)
- PSLV C26/IRNSS-1C launched successfully (16 October)
- GSAT 6 launched successfully with Ariane-5 from Kourou (7 December)

- LVM 3-X/CARE Mission, experimental suborbital recovery mission, carried out successfully (18 December)

2015
- PSLV C27/IRNSS-1D launched successfully (28 March 28)
- PSLV C 28/DM C3 launched successfully (10 July)
- GSLV D6/GSAT 6 with indigenous cryostage launched successfully (27 August)
- PSLV-C30/ASTROSAT launched successfully (28 September)
- GSAT-15 launched successfully (11 November)
- PSLV-C29/TELEOS launched successfully (16 December)

2016
- PSLV-C31/IRNSS-1E launched successfully (20 January)
- PSLV-C32/IRNSS-1F launched successfully (10 March)
- PSLV-C33/IRNSS-1G (launched successfully (28 March
- Reusable Launch Vehicle Technology Demonstrator RLV-TD launched successfully (23 May)
- PSLV-C34/CARTOSAT-2 launched successfully (22 June)
- ISRO Scramjat Engine Technology Demonstrator successfully launched (28 August)
- GSLV-FOS/INSAT-3DR launched successfully (8 September)
- PSLV-C35/SCATSAT-1 launched successfully (26 September)
- GSAT-18 launched successfully (6 October)

Annexure 2

Indian Spacecraft

Communication Satellites: Supports telecommunication, television broadcasting, satellite news gathering, societal applications, weather forecasting, disaster warning, and search and rescue operation services.

Earth Observation Satellites: The largest civilian remote sensing satellite constellation in the world – a thematic series of satellites supporting a multitude of applications in the areas of land and water resources, cartography, and ocean and atmosphere.

Scientific Spacecraft: Spacecraft for research in areas like astronomy, astrophysics, planetary and earth sciences, atmospheric sciences and theoretical physics.

Navigation Satellites: Satellites for navigation services to meet the emerging demands of civil aviation and to meet the user requirements of positioning, navigation and timing based on the independent satellite navigation system.

Experimental Satellites: A host of small satellites mainly for experimental purposes. These experiments include remote sensing, atmospheric studies, payload development, orbit controls, recovery technology, etc.

Small Satellites: Sub 500 kg class satellites – a platform for stand-alone payloads for earth imaging and science missions within a quick turnaround time.

Student Satellites: ISRO's student satellite programme aims to encourage various universities and institutions for the development of Nano/Pico satellites.

Annexure 3

Size of Indian Launchers

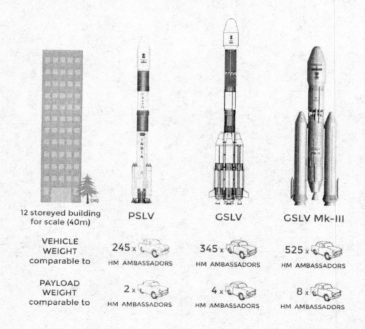

	12 storeyed building for scale (40m)	PSLV	GSLV	GSLV Mk-III
VEHICLE WEIGHT comparable to		245 x HM AMBASSADORS	345 x HM AMBASSADORS	525 x HM AMBASSADORS
PAYLOAD WEIGHT comparable to		2 x HM AMBASSADORS	4 x HM AMBASSADORS	8 x HM AMBASSADORS

Acknowledgements

I would like to begin with a very special thanks to the extended ISRO family with whom I have spent my entire working life and without whose love, support and inputs this book could never have been written.

The events and anecdotes I have penned are part of my personal memory, but the sculpting of the story and the shaping of the narrative has been the work of my wife Gita who has travelled with me on the ISRO journey for most of the half century.

A Brief History of Rocketry in ISRO by my two former colleagues P.V. Manoranjan Rao and P. Radhakrishnan and *India's Rise as Space Power* by former ISRO chairman U.R. Rao were invaluable reference for my research.

The Public Relations Division of ISRO Headquarters provided me with many of the spectacular pictures and other material which I have used in the book.

Some of the other historic pictures came from my own personal collection, which I have carefully preserved over the years.

I owe my biggest debt of gratitude to our friend V.K. Karthika, former publisher of HarperCollins India, without whose persistent egging on I would never have ventured on this rather daunting project.

I would also like to thank our commissioning editor Ajitha G.S. whose smart ideas helped to give the book its contemporary feel.

I owe a big thanks to my two sons Ananth and Sriram, my daughter-in-law Shuba and my grand-daughters Layaa and Meera for their constant love and support.

Index

25 📖 HarperCollins India Ltd

Celebrating 25 Years of Great Publishing

HarperCollins India celebrates its twenty-fifth anniversary this year. Twenty-five years of publishing India's finest writers and some of its most memorable books – those you cannot put down; ones you want to finish reading yet don't want to end; works you can read over and over again only to fall deeper in love with.

Through the years, we have published writers from the Indian subcontinent, and across the globe, including Aravind Adiga, Kiran Nagarkar, Amitav Ghosh, Jhumpa Lahiri, Manu Joseph, Anuja Chauhan, Upamanyu Chatterjee, A.P.J. Abdul Kalam, Shekhar Gupta, M.J. Akbar, Satyajit Ray, Gulzar, Surender Mohan Pathak and Anita Nair, amongst others, with approximately 200 new books every year and an active print and digital catalogue of more than 1000 titles, across ten imprints. Publishing works of various genres including literary fiction, poetry, mind body spirit, commercial fiction, journalism, business, self-help, cinema, biographies – all with attention to quality, of the manuscript and the finished product – it comes as no surprise that we have won every major literary award including the Man Booker Prize, the Sahitya Akademi Award, the DSC Prize, the Hindu Literary Prize, the MAMI Award for Best Writing on Cinema, the National Award for Best Book on Cinema, the Crossword Book Award, and the Publisher of the Year, twice, at Publishing Next in Goa, and more recently, the Publisher of the Year Award 2016 at Tata Literature Live, Mumbai.

We credit our success to the people who make us who we are, and will be celebrating this anniversary with: our authors, retailers, partners, readers and colleagues at HarperCollins India. Over the years, a firm belief in our promise and our passion to deliver only the very best of the printed word has helped us become one of India's finest in publishing. Every day we endeavour to deliver bigger and better – for you.

Thank you for your continued support and patronage. And here's wishing everyone a great new year!

HarperCollins*Publishers*India

🐦 @HarperCollinsIN

📷 @HarperCollinsIN

📘 @HarperCollinsIN

in HarperCollins Publishers India

www.harpercollins.co.in

Harper Broadcast

Showcasing celebrated authors, book reviews, plot trailers, cover reveals, launches and interviews, Harper Broadcast is live and available for free subscription on the brand's social media channels through a new newsletter. Hosted by renowned TV anchor and author Amrita Tripathi, Broadcast is a snapshot of all that is news, views, extracts, sneak peeks and opinions on books. Tune in to conversations with authors, where we get up close and personal about their books, why they write and what's coming up.

Harper Broadcast is the first of its kind in India, a publisher-hosted news channel for all things publishing within HarperCollins. Follow us on Twitter and YouTube.

Subscribe to the monthly newsletter here: https://harpercollins.co.in/newsletter/

▶ Harper Broadcast

🐦 @harperbroadcast

www.harperbroadcast.com

Address

HarperCollinsPublishers India Ltd
A-75, Sector 57, Noida, UP 201301, India

Phone
+91 120-4044800